MW00712139

Twelve Guaranteed Ways To Stay Miserable

(Or Change)

Patricia L. Zerman, MS, LPC
& Beverly J. Wolf

Twelve Guaranteed Ways To Stay Miserable

Published by Atlanta Center for Attitudinal Awareness Publishing

www.~~tacfaa.com~~ aac@atlantaawarenesscenter.com
(770-953-3136)

Atlanta Awareness Center
1373 Old Virginia Ct. SE
Marietta, GA 30067

Copyright TX6-096-831 December, 2004 Atlanta Center for Attitudinal Awareness Publishing. All rights reserved. No part of this book may be reproduced or transmitted in any form or by any means, electronic or mechanical, including photocopying, recording or by any information storage and retrievals system – except by a reviewer who may quote brief passages in a review to be printed in a magazine, newspaper or on the Web – without permission in writing from the publisher. For information, please contact Atlanta Center for Attitudinal Awareness Publishing, 2900 Delk Road/Building 700/Suite 128/Marietta, GA 30067.

Although the author and publisher have made every effort to ensure the accuracy and completeness of information contained in this book, we assume no responsibility for errors, inaccuracies, omissions or any inconsistency herein. Readers should use their own judgment or consult a therapist for specific applications to their individual problems. Names, characters and incidents are fictitious and are not to be construed as real. Any resemblance to actual events, locales, organizations or persons, living or dead, is entirely coincidental.

First printing December, 2004
ISBN 0-9763136-4-2

Cover Design by Publication Services
Illustrations by H.C. Clements
Graphic Design by Adam Lenio
  Rick Presley & Mark O'Malley
Edited by Pam Ryan
  & Phillip Bellury

"The story of Rutgar and Rocky is about a new way of looking at the world and yourself. Patricia Zerman cleverly and entertainingly gives you practical and easy to understand tools that can apply to every aspect of your life. The cartoons and the large print make for easy reading. If you want to get rid of being miserable and live a life that demonstrates the truth, unconditional love, happiness and peace, this is the book that was meant for you."

Gerald G. Jampolsky, M.D.
Author of Love is "Letting Go of Fear"

TABLE OF CONTENTS

Acknowledgments

This book is dedicated to all of the people who have touched my life and all of the lives I've been allowed to touch. I can't begin to express my deep appreciation and gratitude to everyone who has believed in me and offered their support along the way. Thank you... I trust in my heart you all know who you are!

Introduction

At a critical point in my life I had become totally and completely discouraged as to why I was here and what life was all about.

Thankfully, I was **determined** to find answers and was unwilling to accept misery as an option any more. Even though I felt like giving up and ending it on many occasions, I somehow **knew** there had to be more. Deciding to make "Self-discovery" my number one priority, I began a journey that has never ended. I read lots of books, studied with teachers near and far, listened to a staggering number of tapes and meditated a great deal. Through it all, I've uncovered a tremendous passion and eagerness for life's unlimited potential, which is the basis of what I have been living and teaching for over 15 years.

My journey continually teaches many things. A very important lesson was that painful emotional imprints harden within us and are deeply rooted, like paw prints left behind in a newly poured sidewalk. Mechanical reactions and self-taught rules keep you "stuck." In order to change you must be willing to pour a new layer of emotional cement and let it dry with a smooth surface. As you clear out the cobwebs, so-to-speak, there will be no prints this time, unless of course, you are determined to stay miserable. The intent of this book is to tell you why the world is full of people reacting to ghosts and shadows and how to do something about it. **Everyone has that choice!**

Misinterpretation of situations, which is seeing through a fog of imposed beliefs, is exactly how the negative ego keeps faulty imprints from the past alive. The "**Negative ego**" is defined as that part of our consciousness that doesn't want us to be happy. Similar to the "bad guy" in a movie, it's the part that's determined to keep us miserable by filtering current situations through what's already taken place, those pre-recorded prior experiences that distort what's happening now. I opened myself up to change and stopped listening to the negative ego... enough so, that I found a way out of misery.

Recently there was a story in the newspaper about a lady in California who had a large lump on her back, similar to that of the Hunchback of Notre' Dame. A surgeon offered to remove it at no cost to her, including the hospital fee. Initially she accepted this gracious offer. The night she checked into the hospital, preparing herself for the surgery, she called the doctor with a sudden change of mind. She told him she couldn't do it. He asked, "Do you mind telling me why? I told you everything was free and there was no obligation on your part." She said she was sorry and told him she had lived so long with that large lump she didn't think she could go on without it.

People don't seem to be able to live without their deep-seated painful imprints any more than she could live without her large lump. Society is so used to perpetuating, expecting and accepting misery that it seems almost impossible to accept the fact that things can be otherwise. Thank God for shows like Oprah and Dr. Phil, which help individuals realize there are other options.

Successful author and screenwriter Susan Jacobsen summarized it well, "Few people believe that they are entitled to more than a few hours of happiness a week. A short spell of happiness, accentuated with suffering the rest of the time, is not what you're here to experience."

Is the truth too good to be true for you? Find out! Start your change process by reading the following pages and see where it takes you. You have nothing to lose and everything to gain!

RUTGAR'S STORY...

<u>PART I</u>

It was a cold, dreary winter afternoon, way too nippy for venturing out. Rutgar settled into his well-worn cozy leather chair. Outside the big picture window there was a fresh layer of snow blanketing the ground. Listening to the comforting crackle of the warm fire he smiled lovingly as he watched his dog Rocky sleep, twitching painfully while experiencing some sort of bad dream. Wanting to help he reached down giving Rocky a gentle shake, waking him from his self-induced predicament. "Most people wish life were that easy," he thought "...to be able to leave a frightening situation that quickly and be in a better place. **It is**, but of course nobody believes that!" In a split second Rutgar flashed back to a scary place he once investigated, a place called Misery...

Rutgar is a detective, a **great** detective! He's been a natural born snoop all his life. It's no wonder he grew up to be a well-respected and much sought-after private investigator. Rutgar's curiosity and how far he'll go to satisfy it are legendary. Before he can relax, the guy absolutely **has to know** what makes people tick, what goes on behind the scenes and why things happen.

He can't stop wondering why people do the crazy things they do and is continuously amazed by the antics of their repeated messes. The outlandish schemes dreamed up by some of his clientele read like a novel. He studied loads of self-help material, read books about the brain and took night courses in psychology

and sociology at the local university trying to get to the bottom of this. Being an investigator has given him loads of first hand experience. His files prove it!

Case after case comes in from clients finding themselves in crisis situations spurred on by the drama they've created in their own lives. Feelings are avoided, lies are told to manipulate those around them, then fear and anger set in and these people end up in trouble and in need of assistance. It's a nightmare. They call hoping Rutgar can get them out of it, which of course he does. The sad part is that by wanting **him** to fix them they **avoid** working it out on their own. Rutgar keeps busy primarily from repeat customers. They never seem to learn from the previous situation he's pulled them through.

"Rocky, if people only believed they were valuable enough to face their problems, follow their intuition and speak up, I'd be out of a job in no time," he laughed. So it's no wonder with all the hoopla he heard about a place called "Misery," he felt compelled to investigate. "My intuition tells me that something here is not right," he murmured to himself, "and my intuition has never failed me yet. The perplexing thing about Misery," he said to himself, "is that so many people live there. They all say they want to leave, but rarely do. Why is that?"

Rutgar wanted answers and decided to check things out for himself. His preliminary research showed him that the number of recorded complaints on file were astronomical. He put all his projects on hold, printed directions from the Internet, got Rocky, packed up the car and bravely drove off.

They had no idea what they were going to find when they arrived, but were prepared for the worst. After all, nothing good had ever been said or heard about this place. One thing he knew for sure... that whether they have visited Misery or not, people know its reputation as an awful place to live. Being a devoted private-eye, he was sure that the more he knew about Misery the more skilled he would be at problem solving in the future.

Arriving in Misery was a shock! Rutgar immediately got a creepy feeling in the pit of his stomach. The situation was worse than he had suspected. People walked as if they had the weight of the world on their shoulders. Nobody smiled. Everyone seemed to be on edge and suspicious. The air was filled with a tangible sense of grief and despair, far more than he first imagined. As he let his eyes roam, canvassing the scene, he couldn't help but notice a huge sign at the city's entrance. **No one could miss this!** Rutgar's face turned ashen as he read it. Rocky buried his head under his paws after seeing the expression on his master's face. He gasped as he studied the words:

Rutgar let out a nervous laugh. "Surely this must be a joke," he said to Rocky. But the terrified look on his face and the squeamish feeling in the pit of his stomach made him believe otherwise. Rocky huddled closer, not sure what to make of it all. Rutgar cautiously drove on, noticing the Welcome Center directly ahead. He parked out front and gathered all the courage he could muster, determined to go inside. He needed cold hard facts about this dismal place and wanted to see those "Rules & Regulations" spelled out. Maybe he could figure out just what he was dealing with.

As Rutgar reached for the door Rocky started shaking. Rutgar was certain the poor fellow did not want to be left alone, but animals were not allowed inside. He tenderly reassured his loyal companion he would be back in a flash.

The "Welcome Kits" were piled high on a desk similar to those found in hotels. No one said hello or greeted him. It felt eerie. A simple piece of paper with a crude arrow pointed to what he was looking for, so he quickly picked up a packet and flew out the door. Rocky's tail wagged as fast as it could go as Rutgar opened the car door to jump in. After reassuring Rocky everything was okay and nestling down in the seat, he started reading the following disturbing regulations… purposefully visualizing himself in each role to get a better perspective:

Official Welcome Kit

Rules &
Regulations
For Living In
Misery

Compliance Mandatory

Introduction

Within the contents of these pages you will find "Twelve Guaranteed Ways to Stay Miserable" which we, the Mayor and the City Council, voted into ordinances that must be followed to live in Misery. The population is growing at a staggering pace therefore it is imperative that these Rules & Regulations be strictly enforced or you cannot remain here. Many people find comfort living in Misery. Make sure you are not left out. Be aware, offending parties will be dealt with summarily.

The Mayor and City Council

1) Never Be Selfish
(With A Capital "S")

In Misery we encourage people to walk all over each other. We feel that individual wants and needs get in the way of being a miserable citizen. It's necessary to give up your own personal interests for the sake of others to live in Misery. Abiding by this rule should be easy... we're sure you've done it before. It's not a big adjustment. Simply put, you never come first. Your wants and needs don't count. You're not important. We find it's helpful to use the analogy of being a **doormat** when memorizing it.

To assist you further in complying with this first rule, we request that you keep your intuition at bay. In fact, never follow it. Instead, ignore any kind of direction or warning signs it sends out. Go against, argue with and fight those dastardly tugs in your tummy. Intuition separates the hopeful from the hopeless. It takes care of you. This would alienate you from the rest of those living in Misery and you wouldn't want to stray from the pack. We want to enforce uniformity in Misery, that's why we've adopted "Misery Loves Company" as our town motto.

We've handily constructed the rules to neatly piggy-back off each other. They lend unparalleled support to helping you lose sight of who you are by encouraging you to continuously go against your personal needs and desires. Saying "yes" when you mean "no" and "no" when you mean "yes" makes it simple to conform to all twelve of Misery's Regulations. You'll see how this first rule cleverly paves the way for the other eleven. To properly begin the process, subscribe to our local paper "Daily Eruptions". This starts the day off right by guaranteeing seismic shakeups of varying size and proportion. Join the crowd by not rocking the boat and it's certain you'll help keep misery alive and well!

2) Avoid and Pretend

This is a sure-fire way to max out emotionally and make your stay in Misery all the more perplexing. Avoid and ignore all those emotions that make you feel crazy and sick inside by pretending that everything is okay when it isn't. It sort of feels like not studying for an upcoming test or keeping your mouth shut when you want to scream, according to most residents.

You'll find these two types of denial make it easy to live in Misery by causing endless nights, illness, unhappiness, nervousness, relentless uneasiness, weight gain/loss, loads of frustration and irritation... not to mention ulcers... just to name a few. Sound appealing? It gets better. Depression is one of the grander returns accompanying this method of coping. Repeated denial of true feelings propels agony to new heights. How do you think you found this place?

The Ostrich Syndrome has much to offer with assisting you in perfecting this rule. That's why it's our second pick. Keep pretending no one can see you while your head is stuck in the sand. Next, brace yourself for a swift kick from behind. Be ready to suffer constant setbacks from all those emotions you say don't exist. Avoiding and Pretending make being miserable a no-brainer. Give it a try! And don't forget our motto, "Misery Loves Company!

3) Stay Immobilized in Fear

A great way to live miserably is to be controlled by fear. Refuse to confront uncomfortable situations head on. Whatever you do, don't take the necessary steps to walk through them. Count on endless suffering by running away from what scares you. Why worry about having the courage to face fear? Fear gains more power, becoming quite insurmountable and even bigger when you don't. And, as we all know, bigger is better! Live with dread and become hopelessly incapacitated instead. Since Avoiding & Pretending leads to fear, it has to follow in our carefully organized list of regulations and no doubt helps emphasize our motto, "Misery Loves Company".

The thing that makes fear so much fun is that it's self-manufactured, meaning you do this to yourself. So take the time to be imaginative... this way you can dream up so many unrealistic fears you're too scared to make a move. We have a catchy slogan that is a convenient reminder of how unrealistic fear is: False Expectations Appearing Real. You'll soon see the benefit in this.

But wait... there's more! Fear's intensity magnifies each time it's rehashed. Recollecting the bits and pieces neatly puts them back together again. Make sure to beat yourself up by creating scarier revisions. Keep past worries and reactions close at hand. This makes for tantalizing scripts filled with loads of panic and uncertainty. You're both writer and director rolled into one. What a grand scheme for creating frightful scenarios! Just think of the opportunity you have to become a star in Wallow Wood – Misery's very own version of Hollywood. The cameras are rolling. That's exciting entertainment you won't want to miss!

4) Lie to Yourself and Others

Liars are welcomed and encouraged in Misery. Be certain you join them. Lying quadruples worthlessness, a highly sought-after result here. You've lied to yourself enough over the years. It's time to share the fun!

Like wildfire, lies destructively spread and build on themselves. Liars live in a very small world and automatically assume everybody lies like they do, so they never trust or believe anyone. Life is shaky and unsettling at best. That's what living in Misery is all about. No doubt, the constant upheaval certainly keeps you walking on eggshells. There's an additional perk... trying not to forget the lies already told! It's very exhilarating and leads to loads of anxiety. Misery mounts exponentially.

We think it's fascinating to watch people use their vivid imaginations to create chaotic worlds for themselves just like the 'script and movies' idea described in Rule #3. Reality is overrated. It's fun to see residents squirm from getting caught up in the layers of lies it takes to cover themselves. We do not value trust in Misery and find it offensive when people speak truthfully. The truth hurts therefore we prefer fantasy to facing any pain caused by telling the truth. We hold conventions for the anxious and untrustworthy with incredible turnouts. You should consider attending because "Misery Loves Company!"

Lying may not be your strong suit, therefore we believe it's best to start with little white lies and work up to the big whoppers. For **maximum** benefit we suggest lying to your heart's content. There's tremendous value in this one. Don't pass it up!

18

5) React and Become Defensive

Have you ever considered living life as one big sore spot? Becoming one of the walking wounded instills touchiness beyond belief and has its own rewards. When offered any form of constructive criticism, be reactionary. Make sure to lash out at others for the emotional wounds you carry and definitely be defensive. Don't bother listening to or digesting what others say to you either.

When you feel raw and upset, rather than discovering why words or actions knock up against you, become numb and feel damaged. Take it personally and develop extreme sensitivity. Maintain a shield of blame. Stay puffed up, brittle and sore. Sulking and pouting are beneficial, too! There's nothing more miserable than walking around like a huge pincushion. No doubt, you will fit right in with our crowd.

Keeping a scowl on your face also helps. We offer scowl-training classes for those who have not perfected the "right look" in conjunction with Misery's requirements. If you aren't into group classes, a case of severe sunburn conveniently serves as a vivid example of what we are trying to convey… you do not want anyone to come close. As one of the amenities, we offer a great place to sunbathe. Visit our private beach at Lake Woeisme. You can pick up a thing or two from the downtrodden residents who bask in resentment and hang there. They delight in our motto, "Misery Loves Company!"

6) Rationalize, Analyze and Stuff Everything

It's a sure bet that any time you are rationalizing or analyzing you are thinking. Thinking is a **spectacular** way to stay miserable, while appearing quite innocent. Dwelling on trials and tribulations captivates the mind by redirecting and diverting emotions. This makes you look like you are really smart because you have an intellectual advantage. Since you can't think and feel at the same time, rationalizing and analyzing allow you to temporarily reroute what's actually going on.

We are well aware that thinking profoundly multiplies problems. If you've overlooked that point, reread Rule #2. It's a wolf in sheep's clothing... exactly how misery thrives and stays alive. Stuffing problems away by rationalizing and analyzing them to death helps produce anxiety, pressure and stress. Add constant agitation as well. The turmoil never stops. You can't get rid of it! Use this technique if a lot of tossing and turning are on your agenda. As a fabulous bonus you'll be uptight, touchy, irritable and out of sorts... all key requirements for living in Misery.

Stay locked in your head. The resulting tension will build up and, like a volcano you'll explode before you know it. By the way, this is the ticket to that long-awaited nervous breakdown you've anticipated for years. While you're waiting don't forget our motto, "Misery Loves Company!"

7) Point One Finger Out
(Ignore the Three Pointing Back)

This is a little trick that keeps you from taking **any** responsibility, a terrific way to escape reality and be **terminally** dependent on blame. As long as you are convinced that the root cause of any problem is somebody else, rest assured that moving out of Misery is not an option. This is what you're really hoping for, isn't it? If you work at total abdication of ownership for everything, you can develop an amazing ability to justify why it's always someone else's fault. Refusing to be held accountable is a marvelous way to drag out suffering for eons and also why pointing the finger is quite a featured talent of our residents.

To maintain your status in Misery and uphold the covenants properly, we ask that you follow this rule carefully. It's mandatory to keep that index finger armed, cocked and ready to point at anyone but yourself. Never acknowledge or bother to accept that it's **you** who are feeling, seeing and hearing the problem. Point... don't pause. Use that finger to make it clear to everyone that your issues are continually someone else's fault. If you can't find fault, react and become defensive as explained in Rule #5. Any semblance toward possession of a problem leads to the dissolution of it and we don't want that. Finger pointing is considered a highly developed skill and an asset here in order to live by our motto, "Misery Loves Company!"

8) Manipulate & Have Motives

Tired of not getting what you want? Join the club! In Misery we pride ourselves on taking charge of our destinies through manipulation.   When you aren't getting what you desire, manipulation is a viable solution to your dilemma. You want results **now**! Unless you can manipulate the situation, you're afraid you'll never get what you want. Have it your way! That's the spirit we like here. It's more stimulating anyway. Manipulating yourself or others to circumvent the truth isn't honest and it **will** keep you busy.

Make manipulation a priority. It's a significant part of sustaining a high-quality life in Misery. You'll never stop feeling discouraged if you take our advice, especially when manipulation is loaded with lots of motive. This is tied directly to Rule #4. As the finishing touch, add a few small lies or one big doozie to top off your game plan. Just like putting a cherry on top of a chocolate sundae!

Of course, manipulation never works and you end up being more miserable. Well, that's the point of living in Misery, right? But you never know, you might become famous. You've seen all the reality shows. First-rate drama comes from manipulation. When you least expect it, one of our well-known TV scouts might be right around the corner waiting to catch you in action. Pitch in and do your part. After all, "Misery Loves Company!"

9) Swim In Guilt & Carry The Burdens of the World

This rule probably requires little or no explanation. Where would Misery be without guilt? Come on, most likely you were fed on it like milk from your mother. How would we know how to discipline our children, let alone ourselves, if it weren't for guilt? Guilt destroys many lives. It's subtle and generally goes undetected for years, feeling more like a mild annoyance than the destroyer it is. It's a favorite rule... considered one of Misery's most popular.

Whether you are trying to control yourself or someone else is working hard to control you, there are lots of should haves, could haves, or ought tos involved... providing you with plenty of excuses to swallow shame. Guilt stems from doing something you felt was wrong but did anyway. You feel bad, like scum, but won't admit it. We like that in Misery. It's intimidating and keeps residents in their place.

Ha-ha! Those heavy, ingrained feelings of duty, obligation and responsibility build relentlessly. They become ominous foreboding emotions, sort of like waiting for a tornado to touch down. The aftermath leaves quite a mess in its trail. You'll feel worn out from carrying that overwhelming sense of inevitable punishment. If being locked in depression is a life-long dream, guilt is the perfect nightmare to make your dream come true. Don't wait to put this one into practice. We want you here because as you know: "Misery Loves Company!"

10) Hold Onto Your Anger, Resentment and Blame

Do you dream of aspiring to everlasting victim-hood? One powerful way to absolutely ruin your life is to hang onto anger and resentment. Make sure to blame everyone in your life but you for what's happened. **OF COURSE** it's not **your** fault. How could it be? You had nothing to do with coming into this life. It's your parents' fault. How you live is definitely based on the others around you, especially your uncaring boss, insensitive friends and unfeeling spouse. Not getting what you want isn't a shortcoming of yours by any means. If it doesn't work it must have something to do with outside forces, not self-imposed limitations.

For best results the City Council suggests you follow this plan of action: 1) Be unreasonable when you don't get what you want; 2) feel out of control; 3) project those feelings onto someone else and 4) refuse responsibility. Clever tactics aren't they?

There's no better reward than having a tantrum, stomping your feet and throwing a fit! We support this behavior by inviting you to our annual Bellowing Ball, which comes in the middle of January when the world is gray. It's a perfect setting for making and breaking New Year's Resolutions too.

At this Grand Gala we proudly offer the rare opportunity to justify rage by projecting all the damage you've experienced onto others. What a relief! Utter misery is yours for the taking. In addition this affords the luxury of refusing to believe that you have any part in your own destiny. That's why we celebrate this special occasion and there's no better time to rehearse our motto, "Misery Loves Company!"

30

11) Worry

Worry is a fabulous way to stay immobilized in Misery. You get to feel paranoid, live in constant fear and continually experience life as a perpetual guessing game. For improved results we insist you speculate needlessly. Worrying keeps you removed from yourself, diverting discomfort by endlessly picking things apart. This offers a false sense of control and is acceptable as a first line of defense. But in truth worry is only a way to con yourself into believing you can ditch fear of the unknown by thinking things to death. Nausea is a constant factor from living in the past or projecting into the future, adding additional appeal. That's why worry was chosen as Rule Number Eleven. It's a dramatic mind trick assured to draw attention straight to insecurities, doubts and fears. Heavy sighs add to the effect.

Furthermore, your pronouncement of good or bad, right or wrong actually makes you believe your senseless judgment has relevance. Anyone who judges stands self-judged. Feel free to join the "What If" league. They meet weekly to practice projection. Those that master this feat project till it hurts and faithfully uphold our motto, "Misery Loves Company". There's no end in sight to the amount of suffering or problems you'll develop. Worry perpetuates itself, so have at it. Feeling trapped in a never-ending time warp of paranoia is like living in your own made-to-order haunted house. Composed entirely of fanciful stories this allows that all-consuming "non-sense," that has nothing to do with the here and now to take over. The unending chaos is mind-boggling, a must for living in Misery!

12) Don't Ever Risk

Can't stand anything new because you don't like things being out of the ordinary? We proudly promote procrastination! Don't risk, that way you won't feel threatened by change... and isn't that the reason you were drawn to Misery? Not risking is indisputably and unquestionably a lack-luster way to stay miserable. There's no need to worry about ever feeling disoriented or facing anything new and frightening. If living in a rut is your heart's desire, you've finally found something that leads to satisfaction.

You are free to live an uninspired, dreary, mundane existence forever. Try new things? Hogwash! Act like a possum and play dead. The enticing compensation package you'll receive from refusing to risk consists of; no excitement, a remarkable ability to make excuses, an abundant resistance to spontaneity, feeling alone and empty. Let this be your slogan: "If I don't risk, I can't exist".

Not risking leaves you constantly wondering why you're on the planet. Miserable and melancholy just about sum it up. It creates an astonishing life full of mediocrity. Not risking change allows you to procrastinate as long as you like, bringing life to a halt. Refer back to Rules #2 and #6 for help. You'll see that this puts closure on all twelve rules. One that offers an illustrious opportunity for solid footing in Misery and assures you that you won't leave any time soon. As you know, "Misery Loves Company!"

Summary of
<u>Rules</u> & <u>Regulations</u>
For Living In Misery

Surrender To Helplessness
And Become Hopeless

If the "Twelve Guaranteed Ways to Stay Miserable" stated herein have not created a clear picture of what you are required to do to live in Misery, then we suggest putting into practice our last option "Surrender to Helplessness and Become Hopeless". This option includes all the others but takes living in Misery a step further. Noted to be very destructive, it's the best way to take living in Misery to another level. When all else fails, simply give up on life. Don't consider there's a chance. This option affords the unabashed ability to feel sorry for yourself, close your mind to possible solutions, be a victim and use every trick in the book to justify your plight. "Poor me" sums it up perfectly. Using this formula it's next to impossible to remove yourself from the rut of self-condemnation. **Count on it!**

We in Misery have discovered that it's a whole lot easier to throw in the towel than it is to accept responsibility for how the mess got started in the first place. We feel it's too logical to ask for help or do a little digging around inside to see where our feelings of self-defeat and worthlessness began. We aren't interested in doing any work to identify what ill-fated beliefs are blocking us or doing any emotional house cleaning. We don't want to be freed from the trap we're in... that's contradictory to the purpose of living in Misery.

Instead, stay cemented in self-pity blaming the world and everyone in it dropping into a bottomless sinkhole of depression. At this stage we never accept for an instant there's a possibility of climbing out. That way helplessness and hopelessness can go along merrily, hand in hand... it's a method proven by many. You're bound to be totally satisfied with this option if self-destruction and Misery are part of your plan. We take pride in maintaining and wholeheartedly upholding the town motto, "Misery Loves Company" for our residents and ourselves. Don't be left out!

The Mayor and City Council

HAD ENOUGH MISERY?

PART II

Rutgar was dumbfounded by what he read and furiously threw the Welcome Kit into the back seat. "Why in the world would anyone want to live that way?" he asked out loud. Rocky barked eagerly in agreement. Though he chuckled as he saw himself in each role, Rutgar never let any problem get the best of him or take over for too long. He didn't mind asking for help when necessary. "Why suffer?" He did not relish the idea of powerlessness and chose to build self-reliance wherever possible. Watching many of his favorite clients dig themselves into holes made him well aware of the consequences.

He was amused that people struggle with change. Change is a constant fact of existence. In his own life he'd come to realize the disruption or chaos created from transition helped him learn the most. That is, when he was willing to let himself be open and work it through. Actually, he realized that when the dust settled a surprising gift was always left behind. It wasn't easy to ride stuff out, but he was certain his solution was much better than living in Misery.

His face broke into a smile as he was reminded of a cute story that often helped him deal with issues around disappointment and disillusionment. One Christmas two young girls were furiously opening their presents. As one of the little girls opened a gift with her name on it she discovered that the inside of the box was filled with manure. The other youngster looked over totally surprised and said, "Yuck… that's not a present!" The little girl opening the box said, "Wait a minute. No so fast. Who says it's bad? There's got to be a pony in here somewhere".

WHICH ONE ARE YOU?

Rocky had been very patient while Rutgar read through the Welcome Kit. His head was stretched over the seat nuzzled in Rutgar's lap. It was time for a well-deserved break. A quick walk before heading back home would do the trick. Car doors locked, they headed toward the town square and came upon a strange sight to behold. There, in the middle of the courtyard too tall to miss, was a gigantic clock tower with all "Twelve Guaranteed Ways To Stay Miserable" on its face. He couldn't believe it! What an unmistakable landmark. The Mayor and City Council made it undeniably clear those "Rules and Regulations" were not to be taken lightly or forgotten while living in Misery.

Rutgar automatically visualized himself as each character again, knowing he had been every one of them at some point in his life. Actually all of them many times, but he genuinely **knew** choosing to stay trapped in any of those roles was no way to live.

He didn't like it here and was ready to leave. Shaking his head in disbelief, he reached down, lovingly stroked his trusted partner and told him it was time to go. "Let's run," Rutgar yelled as they raced back to the car. "We've had our fill of this disgusting place." Whipping the vehicle around without hesitation he and Rocky high-tailed it out of Misery.

As he stared out at Misery's desolate landscape from the car window, Rutgar couldn't help but reflect on the number of times he had felt crappy throughout his life and how uncomfortable it was. "I am not meant to live in Misery. Every time I'm really down in the dumps there comes a point where I am just 'sick and tired of being sick and tired' and can't take it any more," he said to himself. "I have to do something. There's no doubt it has taken incredible dedication, commitment and determination to get myself out of the emotional potholes I've fallen into," he thought. "Yet, I've never regretted spending time reaching inside myself. Nothing stops me from searching for answers. I feel driven and must relentlessly continue to dig. Thank goodness I broke the spell. I woke up from the bad dream that held me captive and I will no longer accept the hypnotic suggestion that I must suffer," he thought proudly. "What makes me different from the people living in Misery?"

"Life isn't as hard as the citizens of Misery make it out to be," he said to Rocky. "It's a shame they won't doubt, question or challenge the mesmerizing self-persecution imposed upon them," he theorized shrugging his shoulders in frustration. "Unlimited choices and unlimited opportunities are available and they insist things won't ever change. They just accept it as their lot in life."

Obviously, coming to terms with the gravity of the situation in Misery wasn't easy. Not only did Rutgar feel shaken from the heaviness of his experience, he felt discouraged and defeated. Thoughts of those dreaded Rules & Regulations swirled non-stop through his head like a curse. The only recourse he had at this stage was to ask himself the perplexing question, "How is it the hocus-pocus of Misery's mind games fools so many?"

Relieved to be on his way home with Rocky comfortably at his side, thoughts of what he had learned over time from various books, classes, teachers and clients floated through his head. A ray of light broke through. Fate kindly delivered a reprieve, bringing with it a great sigh of relief. "Change is possible. **I know that!**" he confidently told Rocky. His emotions took a turn for the better and in that instant his feelings rapidly switched. Rocky felt excitement in the air and wagged his tail with anticipation.

Out of nowhere a sense of urgent compassion welled up inside. Rutgar felt compelled to share the knowledge and experience he accumulated over the years; the knowledge that helped him survive the terrifying times, the various up and down times, as well as the confusing times in between. The inhabitants of Misery needed shaking up, of that he was certain. He doubted they wanted it, but he sure knew it was time and felt he must do something.

Glancing at the Welcome Kit strewn all over the back seat had initially made Rutgar feel incensed and infuriated... then oddly inspired. "Ha!...'Twelve Guaranteed Ways To Stay Miserable,' what a crock!" At that moment Rocky's keen senses let him know something was up, so he crawled a little closer, snuggling tighter against Rutgar's leg. "You make a good teacher Rocky... isn't that exactly what everyone needs?" Rutgar muttered. "The key is to go inside and risk getting closer to their feelings and emotions without being afraid of them. In other words, accept the challenge of likingthemselves enough to be their own best friends. After all, if you don't like yourself – how can you ever expect to like anyone else?"

The ride home didn't take them nearly as long as it did to get there. Being in familiar territory was a blessing. Without hesitation Rutgar quickly opened the door, Rocky jumped out and they headed straight for his office. He hastily flipped on the lights and frantically started rummaging through the stacks of papers on his desk, in drawers and file cabinets. Finally he found what he was looking for… a notebook… a collection of findings he had accumulated from all his studies. He had given it a catchy title, *"Simple Practical Ways To Get Out Of A Mess or Another Way To Look At Problems"*.

Rutgar was committed. Time to issue a wake up call. He wasn't going to let Misery get the best of him or give up without a fight. A sense of urgency permeated the air. As he rapidly turned the pages he came up with an exciting idea. He would single-handedly write his own Welcome Kit. Instead of this Kit consisting of "Twelve Guaranteed Ways To Stay Miserable" it would state just the opposite, overriding the masters of Misery, the Mayor and City Council. Putting into plain words and addressing each Rule & Regulation one by one, his Kit would describe and explain, "Twelve Guaranteed Ways To Leave Misery Behind".

"When I'm finished," he smirked, looking at Rocky with a devious glint in his eye, "you and I will sneak back into Misery's Welcome Center and replace their kits with ours! Wow! What a clandestine scheme… something detectives live for… and maybe, just maybe, a few lives will change through the course of our actions. There must be some individuals who can't stand it any longer. Those who are finally serious about change and earnestly want a way to wake up from the bad dream of living in Misery… and Rocky, we're going to give it to them!" Rocky barked loudly and jumped at Rutgar's feet with his tail wagging wildly. The overpowering enthusiasm was infectious.

Content with that goal in mind, Rutgar and Rocky enjoyed eating a tasty relaxing meal together. They were exhausted from the day's taxing events. It wasn't long before they headed to bed, jumped under the covers and peacefully drifted off to sleep. A job well done, yet still in its infancy.

Official Welcome Kit

Rules & Regulations For Leaving Misery Behind

Compliance Mandatory

Introduction

Within the contents of these pages you will find "Twelve Guaranteed Ways to Leave Misery Behind" which we, the Mayor and City Council, have voted into ordinances that must be followed in order to get out of Misery. The population is decreasing at a staggering rate therefore it is necessary that these Rules & Regulations be strictly enforced or you will remain here. Fortunately, many people have found comfort leaving Misery. Make sure you are not left out. Be aware, parties who ignore this warning will suffer unnecessarily.

The Mayor and City Council

Chapter 1

Selfishness With A Capital "S"

Not existing easily took first prize as the overriding theme when Rutgar reviewed Misery's Rule #1. Picking up his pen to write, Rutgar heard the words from one of his teachers echoing through his head, "Okay, you say you are 'sick and tired of being sick and tired.' You've finally had enough. You're ready to put an end to the misery, to dump it somewhere because you can't stand that horrible feeling in the pit of your stomach for another minute. You've tried everything but nothing works. Now you're asking where you go from here.

Learn to put yourSelf first in every decision you make. Like it or not, you will come to understand that you are number one. You are all you've got. That means nothing or no one should be more important than you are. *Without you there IS nothing else."* Those words hit the nail on the head. Rutgar knew his teacher was right. "Yep, when you've sunk that low, the answer is simple. It's about learning to be Selfish with a capital "S," which was the exact opposite of Misery's first rule."

Rutgar retrieved his treasured notebook (entitled "Simple Practical Ways to Get Out Of A Mess – Or Another Way To Look At Problems") and reviewed the first chapter he selected to use for his Welcome Kit replacement:

IMPRINTED MESSAGES FROM CHILDHOOD

When you came into this world you were like freshly poured cement. There were no imprints stamped on you anywhere. You were as pure as the driven snow. As you grew up, sometimes life wasn't what you expected. You felt scared, hurt, rejected, angry, alone, and sad... you didn't know what to do with those feelings. Since you were not sure how to get along in this new place, you tried to figure out what actions would bring about the safety and comfort you needed. Influenced

48

by the people in your world, you ended up doing things you didn't necessarily want to at times, but it brought results that pacified others. You learned how to cope.

Coping mechanisms formed imprints in your emotional cement, which dried and became hardened into your personality. They were imbedded, like a paw print left behind in a new sidewalk. They indicated places where **you** learned to give **you** up in order to get along, to settle and to survive. These imprints show you where you have work to do.

Rutgar smiled as he read that part. He certainly had experienced having his share of imprinted demons haunting him. He eagerly read on.

Parents, numerous authority figures and society taught you to be good, to be nice and to do the right thing using boundaries and limitations. Some boundaries were too strict and some not strict enough, which had far-reaching effects into adulthood... making you conform or rebel. You were seldom taught to take care of you. Instead you were taught to mask your feelings for the sake of approval and acceptance. In addition, religions often influence behaviors making you believe that sacrificing for the sake of others is holy and will get you into heaven. They seldom stress the importance of meeting individual needs.

As a child you had to toe the line, but you're not a child any more. It's time to let the pendulum swing the other way. It's your turn to come first now and to identify your own ideals, which includes taking a personal inventory. You must question whether you allow yourself to be primary in your own life... free to be whoever you want to be. You must also learn to give top priority to your wants and desires. It's sad that this type of consideration is automatically directed toward others and not you. You are left by the wayside. This lack of consideration encourages you to believe those people you've cast yourself aside for are more important than you are.

Rutgar cringed. He'd seen this occurring with hundreds of his clients. He knew that just because you're taught something doesn't mean it's necessarily true. He was certain of that. But the question, "How does taking care of yourSelf lead to long-lasting happiness?" was still unanswered. It sounds so selfish; how could this be? He turned the page and bingo! The answer was staring him in the face. `

TAKE CARE OF YOU - FIRST!

Caring for yourSelf first is paramount to lasting happiness. Putting other people first (sacrifice dolled up as exemplary behavior) is backwards. It's exactly how the world has become screwy and distorted. While this is shocking and contrary to what society teaches, it's true. Being self-important and taking care of you is a permanent solution. Anything else is temporary at best. No doubt, initially this sounds odd and appears closer to the commonly understood definition of "selfishness" with a little "s".

Nothing is less accurate. Actually, when you are selfish with a capital "S" you could never be selfish with a little "s" (taking or greedy) because the two can't coexist. They are complete opposites and repel like polarized magnets. If everyone were to be "Selfish," there would be no need to take from another, all would be cared for naturally. Selfishness with a capital "S" tells you to do what is best for you which is honest, genuine and real. It's mandatory if you want a healthy contented life full of peace, happiness and love.

Being "Selfish" means always admitting the soul-based truth about how you feel inside and honoring it, never going against your tummy (that gut feeling that pulls at you or nudges you twenty-four hours a day). Defining this further, it means never giving yourSelf up for the sake of another or being talked into or out of anything. No lying, keeping quiet, being the nice guy or any other adjective that describes self-abuse or self-denial of any kind. In essence, don't default what is important to you to please others or keep the peace. Doing anything else is a lie. Only say "yes" when you mean "yes," and "no" when you mean "no". As a result natural integrity shows through and prospers.

Rutgar thought of the people he knew who lived this way. "Yep, Rocky, those are the people I admire the most. In fact, I think that's ultimately how I became such a well-known and sought-after detective, since I use this type of thinking for everyday living. How about you, ole' boy?" Rocky, who was chasing rabbits in a dream, grunted a little and barely opened his eyes. Rutgar scratched that favorite place behind Rocky's ear and continued reading.

Another important point that is too often overlooked: **Every time you put another person first in your decision-making, you come last.** No matter how hard the rest of the world tries to make you swallow it, coming last doesn't feel right to anyone who is rational. Nor is it how we are designed. Life is based on survival of the fittest not the weakest link. Giving yourSelf up for someone else says, "Your feelings are more important than mine. Therefore, I will defer my wants and needs to yours. I'm not important enough to be noticed, listened to or fulfilled. I don't count."

Rutgar looked down at Rocky, reminiscing; "I remember being teased by the older kids when I was younger. It felt awful. The last one in the boat is a rotten egg. Na, Na, Na, Na, Na, Na," he recalled them teasing sarcastically. He knew full well there wasn't much he could do. He was little and the bigger kids had the advantage.

While putting others first may seem magnanimous on the outside, it makes you feel absolutely miserable and worthless on the inside. As appearances go, it looks impressive. You may even feel like you've temporarily scored some points. The truth is, deep inside you are seething, and whether you know it or not, every time you do this to yourSelf resentment builds. You keep score and don't forget it. Deep down you feel angry and are convinced in order to get along in this world you are supposed to be at the bottom of the totem pole. It's truly a sad state of affairs and it's exactly how people end up in Misery.

Doubt it? Take a serious look at how much internal work is involved in coping with sucking up or keeping the peace. Look at the amount of mental manipulation and self-talk necessary to make giving yourSelf away acceptable. It takes a lot of effort. That gnawing feeling won't leave because something doesn't feel right.

51

Even though socially the scenario looks picture perfect and is supposed to make you feel better, subconsciously, every time you see that person, you are constantly reminded of what you have done to yourSelf… where you don't count…. you are last.

"Ha!" Rutgar shouted out loud. Startled, Rocky leaped up and yelped apprehensively. "Sorry, boy, didn't mean to scare you. It's just that all of a sudden this makes so much sense. This is why people in relationships wake up one day and can't stand to look at each other. I've seen countless couples crumble from exactly this kind of behavior. I've had friends who were close for years. Then out of the blue they become very irritated with each other and they are not able to tolerate the friendship anymore. This is also why people can't stand their jobs, relatives, or anything else that pushes their buttons.

All that giving up, giving up, giving up of your precious Self (in the guise of being a good person, a team player or a respectful child) takes its toll. Inside you're fuming. You end up hating the world, walking around with a big chip on your shoulder, being a martyr, depressed and helpless… can you see it, Rocky?" Rocky rolled his eyes and settled back on his blanket with a sigh. Rutgar laughed at his shaggy little friend and turned the page.

UNREQUITED LOVE

Placing your happiness in anything outside yourSelf relinquishes responsibility and misplaces control. If the desired results don't meet your requirements you're left feeling empty, upset and typically do a lot of screaming and yelling. Though this concept is ridiculous, it's what most people do. You are not, never have been, nor ever will be responsible for the happiness of anyone else. Nor are they responsible for you. When it gets right down to it, too many people try to save others instead of themselves. You wonder why you feel miserable, walk around feeling deflated most of the time desperately hoping things will change… oblivious to the fact you are actually surrendering the outcome of your life to someone else.

On top of that you refuse to disappoint anyone or let your feelings be known, sitting silently by, quietly eating yourSelf up on the inside with anxiety, worry, and fear. You'd rather die than open your mouth. What you aren't aware of is that you do die inside. Most people are the walking dead, living in Misery. Numb, not dealing with their feelings. Not taking responsibility. Self-anesthetizing. It's incredibly apparent that this is the norm from the number of television commercials pushing pills to enable people to cope in society. *"When are you going to stop doubting and begin believing you are the only person worth living for?"* Rutgar got goose bumps as he read that. *There is no one more important than you are. Learning this one way or another is why you're here. Be committed to what matters in your life... you!* **Then act that way.**

GET SERIOUS ABOUT CHANGE

If you are serious about wanting to heal your life and be happy, you must go back into the past. Do a little detective work of your own. Fix any and all incorrect self-deprecating imprints or wounds and pour a new layer of cement. Let it dry completely without any prints this time. Create a new self-image... a brand new you.

In other words, learn to love yourSelf first or you will never be able to sincerely love anybody else fully in any way, shape or form. You cannot give out that which you do not possess. It's impossible because you really don't know what love is until you experience it for yourSelf. You'll aim high and be full of good intentions in relationships, but your overtures are empty and meaningless, without substance. You'll put a lot of effort into keeping another's affection or attention, but it won't be lasting love. It's more along the lines of neediness, approval seeking and manipulation.

The flip side of this coin is that if you don't love yourSelf, you will never truly accept someone loving you. You won't believe them. In effect, they can't give you something you won't give yourSelf. It's impossible to take in what's not real. There'll be a perpetual feeling of uneasiness in the air and you'll seldom feel secure or trusting.

Before long you'll push them away or sabotage the relationship somehow. It's too uncomfortable for you to deal with, makes you squirm, want distance or to run away. It's difficult to be with someone who is able to love you more than you are willing to love **you**. You've probably been there and understand what's being said here.

Rutgar sat back in his chair and reflected. "Sad commentary about the general public, isn't it, Rocky? That kind of behavior gets you nowhere. Reminds me of that thing about the five glasses of water I read in John Bradshaw's book. He's a therapist, you know. Let's see, how did that go?" Rocky gave him one of those "I don't know what you're talking about!" looks, but Rutgar didn't notice. "Oh yeah, you fill a glass full of water then pour its contents into five other glasses. What happens?

The original filled glass ends up empty. You see, Rocky, that's exactly what happens when you believe other people's happiness, wants and needs are more important than yours. You have to quit being the last person on the list. You have to stop all the excuses. Make it your turn. You are not here to be anybody's savior but your own." Rutgar looked down at Rocky. "Who can forget that notable phrase: Physician, heal thyself? I think that's where it originated. I tell you what, sometimes I just want to shout to the world, 'Are you ready to get out of Misery, or not??!!" He looked down at a puzzled Rocky as he turned the page and blurted out "And I'm sure glad I kept this notebook".

When you begin to live life this way it may trip some triggers and piss a few people off. They aren't used to seeing you act differently or hearing you state what you want. It's startling at first, then after a while, as it becomes your reality the people you know have only respect for you. They realize that you have the courage to watch out for your own best interests and aren't afraid. This takes a lot of guts. Most importantly, they trust you for it.

This new version of you is prone to create some unexpected shock, but ultimately the people you know will feel safer. It becomes a known fact that you don't pull any punches or have hidden agendas. The best part is that nobody suffers in the long run. The cards are always laid out on the table and no one is left guessing.

"Reminds me of Mrs. Crenshaw," Rutgar remarked to a snoring Rocky. "She was strict but I've never forgotten her. Her straightforward, no nonsense nature let me know she really cared. If we all lived that way there would be no human doormats, insecurity or self-abuse to deal with. Ah... what a wonderful world that would be... a world where everyone is a winner." Suddenly Rutgar felt a deep gratitude to his teacher for helping him see this for himself. "Let's read this last part and consider what it takes to get started."

GET STARTED NOW

Start by taking a good hard look at how, where and when you give yourSelf up. Specifically, examine the times you sacrifice, surrender authority, are left feeling empty from your own actions or the expectations of others. Don't be afraid to be totally honest. Love, honor and respect yourSelf at all cost, if only on the inside at first. It's what works and makes all the difference in the world! Begin catching the times you go against you. Don't ignore it. Be alert. Stop saying "yes" to someone when you mean "no" and saying "no" when you mean "yes".

Risk. Be direct about where you're "at" emotionally. Don't be mean, just frank and straightforward. Stop letting other people's happiness come before yours. Be brave. Be different. Put an end to the upset and disappointment you live with or at the very least, pay attention to it. There are already too many unhappy people. Make a decision not to be one of them... decide that you've finally had enough and get serious about eliminating the pain and suffering. It's not easy but well worth the effort you're going to expend. Results are quickly apparent. Try it and see.

The Universe can only give what you are willing to open up to and accept. It acts like a faucet, opening or closing in direct proportion to **how you treat you**. Why complain when you can do something about it? Go exploring. Trade your little "s" in for a big "S". Your happiness depends on you!

Rutgar took a deep breath as he read the final words of that chapter and felt truly inspired. He knew he was doing the right thing. "Hey, Rocky, I've got an idea. Let's put together a list that will really help get the ball rolling. This stuff is too good to forget." Rocky still wasn't sure about his master's behavior but he gave his little tail a wag anyway. Rutgar's list included the following:

SUGGESTED STARTING POINTS FOR LEAVING MISERY BEHIND:

1) Risk putting yourSelf first for a change.

2) Go for what you really want rather than settle.

3) Never go against your gut.

4) Say "yes" when you mean "yes," and "no" when you mean "no."

5) Honor your feelings at all times.

6) Be real.

7) Don't operate out of obligation.

8) Always follow your intuition.

Chapter 2

Avoiding & Pretending

Rutgar felt a sense of accomplishment and proudly tossed his furry little friend a treat. With Rule #1 completed to his liking he was ready to tackle Rule #2. He settled in and studied the rule from the Welcome Kit. This rule clearly revolved around the concept of **insignificance.** Rutgar knew that if you truly believed you were significant you would not avoid issues or pretend problems didn't exist. He had heard an analogy from one of his first-rate teachers a while back that summed it up quite well: "Gauze in itself is harmless and cannot hurt you. But, if I were to wrap you in it from head to toe you'd be immobilized and unable to function. That's how depression sets in. You refuse to feel, acknowledge or accept your emotions, stacking them up layer upon layer, then become incapacitated by acting as if what is happening around you doesn't exist."

Rutgar was very familiar with the concepts of Avoiding and Pretending. They both carried a lot of weight with him. "These two culprits are exactly what send a lot of business flowing my way," he murmured to himself. "By pretending issues don't have relevance and avoiding them, most of my clients or the people in their lives get caught up in all kinds of emotional messes… and then the calls flood in," he contemplated as he leaned back in his chair flashing back through various cases.

"What I initially compiled on this subject matter is too valuable to pass up." He picked up the old tried and true notebook, took a sip of the piping hot coffee he'd fixed and began reciting the following stirring words out loud to Rocky. "Perk up your ears," he said to his pal, "these are concepts I jotted down before you came along… words I was fortunate to find at an early stage in my life that made me a

58

much wiser man". Rocky looked up at his master, rolled over and began to playfully toss and turn, wiggling happily as he scratched his back on the floor.

Avoiding and pretending are skills picked up over the years; for some it's an art. Both are resourceful techniques for overlooking or ignoring matters you don't want to deal with. They allow you to believe you're okay when you're not.

Avoidance rears its head in many forms. Excessive exercise, under or overeating, too much drinking, taking drugs, cutting, being a workaholic, addictive sex, gambling and overspending are examples. They are diversions used to anesthetize so you don't feel what desperately needs to be felt, ways to fill the void left from ignoring what's going on inside.

Rutgar discovered it's the fear of rejection that controls avoiders and pretenders. Collectively, the idea of stirring up trouble makes these people act like Mexican jumping beans. They can't sit still because they are too busy avoiding. It's commonly referred to as nervous energy. They continually try to stay one step ahead of their stored up emotions, like internally running a non-stop marathon.

A spontaneous laugh popped out of Rutgar's mouth as he visualized the ostrich example in Misery's Rule #2. The ostrich is a great symbol of avoiding and pretending. "Have you ever seen one Rocky? When frightened, he sticks his head in the sand pretending to be invisible. He believes he is hiding and doesn't realize the rest of his awkward body is totally exposed leaving him vulnerable to attack. It doesn't register that he is standing in plain sight for whatever is stalking him to see. The ostrich doesn't understand that sticking his head in the sand doesn't help at all."

HIDING FROM PROBLEMS DOESN'T WORK

The same holds true in life. You can't hide from your problems either. Nothing goes away by pretending it doesn't exist or by avoiding it. It can't. Why? There is no resolution, no relief. The itch hasn't been scratched. As a matter of fact, every time you avoid dealing with something the mess gets worse. Taking flight increases problems, fighting feeds them and resistance builds them.

You wouldn't run if what you were running from didn't hold some degree of power over you. Right? Only fear makes people want to hide. Dodging an issue only pops up whenever there's an unwillingness to confront it. The crux of the matter is there's too much discomfort to deal with things up front.

Rutgar's eyes detoured from the page as he read a note scrawled in the margin of his book. It was a story he'd jotted down that graphically illustrated what his astute teacher was trying to convey.

Suppose it's early morning. You start to walk out the door, headed for work. Fortunately, before taking the first step you glance down and suddenly see a rattlesnake curled up in front of you. "Agghhh!" you scream inside, not wanting to startle the snake. Your heart is pounding a hundred miles an hour from shock. Feeling terror-stricken and panicky, what do you do?

Would you pretend the snake is not there and continue to walk to your car? Or, would you slam the door and stay at home all day hoping the snake would leave sooner or later? Even if the snake moved, you'd be a slight bit worried about where that little sucker was hiding! Relaxing would be impossible. Fear of an ambush wouldn't leave your mind. Until the rattlesnake is permanently removed you're going to be jumpy and slightly on edge. What matters the most is feeling safe, the sooner the better.

There's no doubt something must be done to get rid of that pesky creature, but this situation is new to you. You're unsure of what to do. Within seconds you grab the Yellow Pages, frantically searching the listings under Varmint Control. Dialing as fast as you can, you call someone to come and physically remove the reptile. You want peace of mind, to feel secure regardless of the cost. Once you know a professional is in charge, you're relieved. Doubt as to the snake's whereabouts is finally eliminated. It took fast thinking on your part and you breathe a sigh of relief as a lasting solution is quickly found. Thus the snake dilemma has a happy ending.

"You'd go right after it, wouldn't you Rocky ole' buddy... or at least make a lot of noise. You're not afraid... cautious, but not afraid. That's what those folks in Misery need to learn... caution, not avoidance." He leaned forward in the chair, took another sip of delicious coffee and carried on.

ACCEPT <u>ALL</u> OF YOU

Controlling feelings and not expressing them, in one way or another, is not accepting part of you. And, feelings are definitely part of you. There is nothing wrong with anger, disappointment, fear or any other feeling, ever! It's what we do with those feelings that makes life appear distorted and produces trouble. Feelings are also spontaneous, not static. It's okay if they throw you unexpectedly. Actually, it's quite healthy. They are to be felt in the moment, allowed to be there, not stuffed and stored away as something embarrassing or undesirable.

Trying to suppress part of the whole is what creates emotional imbalance. The color blue may be preferred to brown. It doesn't make brown a bad color, both serve their purpose in the panoramic color scheme. Without brown the array of colors in the spectrum would not be complete. The same is true for feelings and bears repeating: No particular feeling is good or bad. It's the **judgment** of a feeling that is the stumbling block, making this one right or that one wrong.

FEEL YOUR FEELINGS WITHOUT JUDGMENT

Throughout your life feelings are mechanically judged then routinely categorized according to acceptability. This is sensed early in life, itemized by what is okay or permissible. A common denominator of "shoulds" and "ought-to's" predominates, overriding what is true for you as an individual. Emotions don't go anywhere by pretending they don't exist or filing them away, however. They are like an open wound that goes unattended and becomes infected, festering and contaminating your entire world.

Decisions around "I like or I don't like" are formed instantly according to protocol. The attitudes of others stand firmly in the foreground. Your wants and needs are relegated to the background. You unknowingly disconnect from yourself, creating a distrust of gut instincts. These ingrained reactionary behaviors become so instinctual that you seldom are consciously aware of it happening. This explains why it often feels as if there are two entirely different people living inside: Person "A" who is solely concerned with your best interests, knowing what it wants for itself; and person "B" who continually overrides the truth, slipping back to what's habitually ingrained through prior experiences of life.

"Yep" Rutgar said to Rocky. "From witnessing how my clients act, this is a clear cut description of what people do to themselves out of habit. When you catch a whiff of something you go after it, don't you Rocky? And, you don't give up until you find it." Rocky's tail wagged as fast as it could go from listening to Rutgar's voice. "People ought to be as determined to dig at their problems as you are to track down a scent," Rutgar sighed.

NOTHING HAPPENS BY ACCIDENT

Similar situations repeatedly show up. They offer the opportunity to release stuffed, ignored or repressed feelings not consciously recognized. These valuable experiences indicate emotions that are split off and sorely in need of attention. Nothing happens by accident. You've heard that a million times. Pay attention to patterns. For instance, people constantly come into your life reminding you of others. In that moment, the current personality is not seen. Whoever is in front of you is coated over with the former person's personality traits.

As far as feelings are concerned you **are** experiencing the person from the past as soon as that memory "hooked into" the prior experience. How many times have you said, "You remind me of so-and-so**?**" Learn to recognize and appreciate these attention grabbers, not flee or ignore them.

"Rocky, that makes me think of Mrs. Beasley. I know she's hard for you to forget. That dog of hers could have been your twin, except her dog was severely hearing impaired. Every time she walked in the door she started shouting at you. Scared you half to death. You'd go hide. It's a shame she automatically projected her dog's characteristics onto you without thinking twice. No matter how many times I reminded her that your hearing was okay, she couldn't separate the two of you."

FEAR FACTOR

Procrastinating offers a temporary breather, but avoiding doesn't cut it. Over time, feelings of failure and conflict turn into a silent form of self-rejection grinding away at your quality of life. Face it. In truth, you are afraid of what you don't want to deal with, and it's that which requires addressing.

Why does tackling fear stir up internal conflict? Confrontation scared you at some point. A feeling of dread imprinted itself and you want to circumvent that from happening again. In reality, you do not have the power to emotionally hurt anyone. Nor do they have the power to emotionally hurt you as discussed in Chapter One. It's your reaction to their words that creates the feeling. You have to let it in, no matter how it appears otherwise… nobody else does it to you. You individually act as judge and jury.

Each of us is personally responsible for any damage that occurs. Nobody else has the power or capability to cause pain. You do it to yourself by letting another's words or actions affect you and then point the blame outside. The height of ego is to believe you can emotionally harm another, even though it seems impossible to accept, you simply don't have that power.

FACING PROBLEMS ELIMINATES PROBLEMS

No matter what the emotional price, facing problems and taking constructive action is the only way to permanently rid yourself of them. Avoiding or pretending problems don't exist is really no different than having that poisonous snake outside your door. You can hope they'll go away on their own, but they won't. There is always a constant dread of an attack lurking around. You're forever on edge wondering what's around the corner or when you will be caught off guard. There's no rest.

"That's why you can fall asleep at the drop of a hat, Rocky. You confront everything that crosses your path and I admire that. Why won't humans do that?" Rutgar continued reading to Rocky. The words had greater significance when he heard them being read out loud.

Permanent removal by dealing with whatever is bothering you is the single workable solution. It's the way to experience peace in the face of uncertainty.

Imagine it this way: You are like a strongly energized magnet. Those things you pretend don't bother you or that you avoid are metal filings.

Once you attract the metal filings they stay connected to your magnetic field no matter how swiftly you try to run away from them.

Rutgar thought back to when he found Rocky. The neighborhood bully had tied a string of tin cans to Rocky's tail. Rocky was only a puppy and was terribly frightened by the noise. The faster he ran the more noise it created. No matter which way he turned or where he tried to hide, the cans followed him. Rutgar came to his rescue and removed the string. They've been together ever since. As he looked down at Rocky he felt extremely grateful to have been given such a delightful friend.

It's funny, because a neighbor of Rutgar's had his own run-in with avoidance. Jeffrey tried very hard to avoid a coworker he couldn't stand. Every day he took the stairs in his building to miss having to confront this guy. The man was pushy and spoke with a very harsh tone. Jeffrey felt intimidated and edgy whenever this man crossed his path. He was too threatened to deal with him. Not surprisingly, one day the boss called a mandatory staff meeting. The group was asked to perform team-building exercises, in which everyone was required to participate. Guess who Jeffery's partner was?

Rutgar recalled Jeffrey telling him this story a while back. He liked the way it emphasized the fruitlessness of resisting. "Who was he kidding, Rocky?" He continued on.

TRICK THE MIND INTO SUBMISSION

Rutgar especially liked this exercise about Changing Perception. It's another helpful way to reduce the power of frightful thoughts by lessening their hold ahead of time. He recognized the importance of using everything available to make taking risks easier.

1) Make four columns of equal width sideways on a piece of paper. The heading for the first column is "Anticipated Reaction". The second is "Your Fear". The third is "Middle Ground". Label the fourth column "Ideal Outcome".

2) Bring up a situation that's bothering you and ask yourself, "What's the **worst** thing that can happen?" Mentally walk it through. Scrape up every detail. Make it real.

Don't ignore a single feeling. Write your results under Column One.

3) Go back to the situation and address the **fear** you have around this happening. Why does it make you react? What does it bring up - rejection, fear, anger, being alone, etc? Those results go under Column Two.

4) Next replay the situation, only with an **alternative** reaction. Visualize an outcome that is middle ground or halfway between the worst anticipated reaction and the ideal. Play out the "what ifs." Think of a solution that's not so menacing. Put those results under Column Three.

5) Lastly, open yourself up to an **ideal** outcome, a positive alternative. The way you prefer it to turn out. There are no limits. Be imaginative. This is about **expanding** options, choices and possibilities, not defining outcomes. The goal of this exercise is to settle busy minds and offer a larger field of potential. It also helps to reduce the impact of past memories, current fears and the feelings of immediacy that make you feel anxious.

You are acknowledging and releasing pent up emotions – **safely**. Facing strong feelings is intimidating, so it's wise to continue this procedure until mental images have no oomph... until the adrenaline rush leaves and the idea of repeating the procedure one more time is irritating. It's safer and better to defuse emotions in your mind than be unprepared if they suddenly knock up against you in a real life situation.

DO THOUGHTS HAVE POWER?

Let's address that concern. It's a legitimate one. You've probably heard the sayings "thoughts become things" and "what you fear you feed". People worry that doing this exercise lends additional power to negative thoughts, that by dwelling on them they'll show up... which seems plausible. However, let's explore why this is not so in this context.

Look at avoidance objectively. By avoiding "negative" thoughts, they actually receive extra attention, building significant reinforcement. It's not necessarily conscious. For example, think of all the times you've done exactly what you swore you wouldn't do. Trying to "not" think about something is repression and carries a lot of weight. You become attached by **trying not** to be attached! Visualize the legal Scale of Justice. Which side leans?

Rutgar knew that doing the exercises helps remove the sting by confronting uncertainty in the mind. He used them regularly himself to lessen anxiety... no running... no hiding. Stare the bully dead in the eye. When you suck the power out of fear and lift the fog, problems fade away.

THE WAY OUT

Before ducking out on an issue, question the reason for a detour. A few of the more significant root causes stem from: a confrontation of some sort jogging memories; something making you feel uneasy or exposed; being afraid to express; relegating important feelings to the back burner; or you want to bide some time.

An inspirational quote states, "Pain is the amount of love you withhold from yourself" and it comes from pretending everything's okay when it's not. **Trusting you to act in your own behalf is the real battle**. Address your fears then take appropriate action. That's how bad habits disappear. **As a man named Alan Saporta cleverly put it, "The best way to escape from a problem is to solve it"**.

Don't stop reaching. Improvement lies in facing your issues and the feelings surrounding them. Self-reliance alone breeds the security, independence and confidence necessary to stand firm, unshaken in your beliefs. No one can have faith in you if you don't have faith in yourself. A wise sage once said, "And the day came when the desire to remain the same was more painful than taking the risk to evolve".

SUGGESTED STARTING POINTS FOR LEAVING MISERY BEHIND:
1) Look squarely at what you want to avoid – if only for a few seconds.
2) Don't allow yourself to stuff any emotion – especially through the use of outside diversions previously mentioned.
3) If you want to run, stay. Feel what comes up instead of bolting.
4) Instead of ignoring or hiding, pay attention to what frightens you.
5) Be open to what is before you, instead of abruptly rejecting it.
6) Wishing is a waste of life and is actually a form of avoidance. Make your wants a priority and be proactive.

Chapter 3

Fear

Rutgar had no sooner picked up his pen when a loud "bang" made him jump! He was no was stranger to noise, but not this much racket. Darting into the living room, he saw Rocky sitting innocently with a quizzical look on his face. He hadn't quite made it around the corner while chasing his favorite ball, had run into the television stand and knocked the VCR off. It didn't break, but it scared the living daylights out of Rutgar. "Wow, Rocky, you really frightened me! At least you're okay and so is the VCR." Rocky, delighted he wasn't in trouble, leaped into Rutgar's arms covering his face with kisses.

"What a great lead-in for rewriting Rule #3. I'm actually experiencing nervousness and a racing heart. Man, it takes a lot of energy to live in fear!" Rutgar emphatically acknowledged. "Just think, for people in Misery being scared is a daily occurrence. They won't challenge situations and are waiting forever for the other shoe to drop. Being reluctant to change and **non-confrontational** *conveys that message," he chided, deciding to include a few notable points from "Stand Up To Fear 101," a seminar for scared-y cats.*

You know what it feels like. Remember that time you were shaken by a near-miss collision or took a test without studying? The times when you couldn't calm the butterflies and nervous energy while waiting for a life-altering phone call? Or when you felt rejected by a lover and never discussed it? Each situation was overshadowed with fearful flashes of uncertainty.

Playing mind tricks temporarily helps alleviate some of the pressure, but those churning feelings keep gnawing away and that all consuming grind in the belly is difficult to overlook. Pretending doesn't deter fear's menacing influence at all. In fact, using that tactic is ineffectual. Dancing around what scares the daylights out of you won't make it go away. There's a deep conviction it has strength, power and a life of its own. Some people say fear is the devil in disguise.

FEAR PARALYZES POTENTIAL

Fear clouds judgment, paralyzing potential. Sensible thinking is impossible. Thoughts that are filtered through worry scatter everywhere. It's like seeing the road through a dirty windshield, causing you to see distorted images. Left to its own devices fear consumes everything in its path. The world is a scary place. Threatening thoughts fuel imaginary ideas and self-belief goes up in smoke. Flames of self-doubt spread like a wildfire in a dry forest. When fear is involved it's impractical to make a decision, especially a wise one.

Rutgar felt his spirits drop from writing this section. He couldn't imagine himself living this way. As he started pondering where fear comes from many questions came to mind... he turned to his ever faithful notebook.

You arrive as a blank slate. Therefore, it's a foregone conclusion that fear is picked up along the way and originates from confusion, the confusion of having to face strenuous situations. Especially where circumstances made you feel unsure or afraid because they weren't expected or anticipated. There was no preparation. You weren't skilled to cope, didn't like being out of control and didn't want it happening again. Something was left incomplete, unresolved emotionally, leaving negative impressions behind that were stored in memory. Not understanding how this mechanized process worked created defenses and fear took hold.

FEAR AND AVOIDANCE: THE PERFECT COUPLE

Stuck in a vicious cycle like a rat on a wheel keeps you living in fear afraid of being faced with what you don't want to see. Thinking about fear or running from fear just guarantees you more of it. Rather than dealing with fearful situations most of us learned ways to postpone them... not knowing that putting up a protective shield inadvertently doubles fear's seductive influence. You become your own enabler.

Skirting issues appears safer. The problem is this: "Whatever you fight you feed." Fear is validated, intensified and multiplied the more you run from it. "Skirting," Rutgar chuckled, "makes me think about those frightened kids we watch in the park. They try to hide behind their mothers. Just like you do, eh boy, when we go to the vet. No skirting around that one." Rutgar laughed out loud.

You've probably heard the well-known phrase, "The thing I fear the most I bring upon myself." It's true. What you focus on expands, especially when it's frightening. Pay attention to where the bulk of your thought goes and make certain fear isn't carrying the most weight. Theoretically, each thought is like putting a five-pound rock in your backpack. That's a heavy load to carry and inevitably takes its toll.

MENTAL CONDITIONING

Mental pictures are nothing but conditioned beliefs that must be addressed. Like a movie projector, every morning when you wake up whatever is going on inside shows up outside. Check it out. **Doubt the mind** instead of being run by it. Embrace what scares you. Then, like air leaking out of an inflated balloon, it will disappear.

Rutgar immediately referred back to Misery's Wallow Wood Studio. He had to agree, life is like a movie. People have a choice as to what scenes they play out. The people in Misery are unaware of that fact.

A few years ago Rutgar met a delightful fellow who was training to be an astronaut. Speaking from experience, he explained exactly how we project fears by describing an exercise the NASA astronauts must perform. "Each person is required to stay alone in a bare cylindrical white room for four hours," he said. "After a while you start seeing everything you ever loved, feared or hated. It's so real you can't believe it's only a mind projection, that it's not something actually there before your eyes."

70

"I kept my sanity by continually remembering the room was empty, which came in handy when snakes appeared. Then I saw my mother, who was so real I reached out to touch her, though logically I knew she died a few years earlier."

This experience clearly illustrates how we project what we believe onto others and the world. It's like playing a Virtual Reality game without knowing it or being hypnotized and not having the trance removed. The astronaut understood the full meaning of, "It's an illusion". This is similar to a scene in the movie "The Matrix", where Keanu Reeves' character stands before a white backdrop and says, "Nothing is real".

IS IT GOOD OR BAD?

Rutgar recalled the renowned and highly acclaimed William Shakespeare who aptly said, "Nothing is good or bad, thinking makes it so".

How do you know, **really know**, if something is good or bad? It's interesting how fast people make that call. Outcomes are typically judged by what's desired the most or deemed the safest. Clearing out imprints depends on embracing the unknown, staying open and evaluating both sides for a change. Most situations hold equal potential for good or bad. Think back to those times when doing what you resisted forced you to take the biggest leap, and, offered the greatest reward.

What you learned love and life to be is a product of your upbringing. You'll automatically seek out, attract and **recreate** what you know, or you'll constantly be on the run from it. It's natural, not good or bad. If you were raised in Italy, you'd speak Italian, be comfortable with Italian people, culture and customs. Life is easier being with people like you. It's already encoded in your emotional circuitry.

"A fossil is a perfect visual example of how fearful notions harden and turn into solidified patterns. They act as a blueprint for handling life. That's why the word FEAR is now an acronym for: False Expectations Appearing Real," Rutgar sighed. He always liked the fossil analogy and used it to get through rough times. "I'd rather work through situations than leave imprints behind," he pondered looking over at Rocky contentedly sleeping on the couch. "Now that's a memorable impression!"

71

CLEAN OUT INGRAINED IMPRINTS

He continued flipping through the pages of his notebook searching for an excerpt he saved that best described F.E.A.R. to a "T." As he reread it to refresh his memory he immediately felt motivated. Author William Samuel effectively explains how fear operates: "The personal thinker's experience is based entirely on causes and effects... Effects expected, anticipated and looked for! **He expects and sees what he believes** *... One doesn't see the* **perfection** *of* **NOW** *while out of long habit, continually looking for the effects of prior causes... causes built upon a personal judgment of limitation, lack, dis-ease and imperfection..."*

To stop being afraid clear out fear-based imprints and work to overcome your own mind. Clean house. Distressing habits and the accompanying reactions must be reconfigured. It's time to repave disturbing emotional roads badly in need of repair. Fill the holes with new options and possibilities.

Positive thinking is a beginning, but the intellect can't override or un-convince you of fear. Only **facing** fear ultimately removes it. You have to **know** it's not real through experience. Remember when you thought a monster was under the bed? You had to be shown it wasn't there before you'd actually believe it. Even then, lingering doubt remained when the lights went out. The same holds true today. Ridding your imagination of scary outcomes isn't easy.

"Yep Rocky, I'll never forget the time I didn't close the door tightly and the wind blew it open. You strolled out for a little investigating of your own. I couldn't find you anywhere and was scared to death. Horrible pictures flashed through my head. I was sick to my stomach. I couldn't bear the thought of losing you. It was obvious I had to calm down and get hold of myself. Projecting fearful outcomes only makes fear more intense. I started taking a lot of deep breaths, forced myself to stay 'right now' and realized I had no idea what the future held. It was evident I only had the present moment. Clinging to **NOW** *as my lifeline I stared fear in the face, halfway settled down and kept roaming the neighborhood calling your name.*

*Exhausted, I went home to wait and had a good cry. I decided to trust that you were smart, knew the way home and relaxed. It was hard. The next thing I knew you showed up at the back door, barked and acted like nothing had happened. I was overjoyed to see you and felt immense relief. Gratitude overtook me. I realized this was a gift. You helped me practice staying **NOW** and not panic. It was painful but very enlightening. Something I won't forget. But don't try that again to teach me another lesson!"* Rutgar smiled excitedly and hugged Rocky tightly.

THE <u>ONLY</u> WAY OUT OF FEAR

How can you be free from fear? Quite simply, stop resisting and walk through it. Let it get close. Fear was made your enemy now make it a friend. Dive into what scares you by learning how it derives power and saps you dry. Then witness the powerlessness of it. Thoughts have no substance, no reality. Yet you act as if threatening ideas or frightening images can jump out and attack on their own or do you in on the spot. It's never dawned on you that it's the continual feeding of this behavior that is actually what keeps it going.

Stop dwelling on the drama of the day, feeling compelled to listen to bad news, soaking it up like a sponge. Evaluate what you hear and recognize there is a huge difference between being cautious in life and buying into the fear surrounding it. Fear is a phantom, yet it's clung to as if it's real. The constantly mulling over, worrying and rehashing convinces you it's factual.

Do you value your aches, pains and miseries? That which you place thought and attention on has great value or you wouldn't spend time with it. If a stray animal is not welcome, stop feeding it. The same holds true for the mind. Stop feeding fear and it leaves. Give up newspapers, television, radio and magazines for a while. Then watch what happens. Get a grip on the tricks your mind uses to freak you out and take over. Thoughts come and go like clouds. They aren't permanent. Take dominion over your mind and realize it's a tool, not a dictator.

LEARN TO LIVE IN THE <u>NOW</u>

The first step toward successfully taking charge is learning to live in the **NOW**. Quiet the mind by staying in the present moment. This offers some sorely needed stillness and the ability to focus, in a detached manner, without distraction. Fear can't survive in the here and now. Staying **NOW** ends thinking, which is where trouble starts. It forces that crazy "monkey mind" to shut up and leave you alone and stops the constant leaping from one scary thought to another. (<u>The Power of Now</u> by Eckhart Tolle is helpful with this profound concept.)

In **NOW** there is no thinking, therefore there are no problems. When you're thinking you're not happy. And, when you're happy you're not thinking. Don't think! Force yourself to **STAY NOW**. Concentrate on what is in front of you, **this** moment. The process does work and is to be taken seriously. Act as if you are hanging on the edge of a cliff and cling to **NOW**. It will save your life. Keep yourself there by saying things like, "Now I am brushing my teeth," "Now I am driving my car," "Now I am on the computer," "Now I am talking on the telephone," "Now I am washing my hair," "Now I am petting the dog." Use any statement you can dream up to be **NOW ONLY**.

Why does it work? Staying **NOW** doesn't allow your mind to bombard you with thoughts. It cuts off communication about the past and stops projection into the future. Nothing is harming you this second. You are okay **RIGHT NOW**. Staying **NOW** equals peace. A common statistic states that ninety percent of worry never happens. Yet worry is one of the most forceful weapons in Misery's arsenal.

WHAT'S THE WORST THAT CAN HAPPEN?

The second step is to take something scary and ask, "What's the worst that can happen?" Answer this completely and be thorough. Then take it further, asking, "Okay, then what?" Continue this by again asking yourself "Then what?" And again "Then what?" Do this until you've exhausted every option. The answers will be surprising. You'll also find you have a better grasp on situations than you realized. Give it a try.

For instance, let's say you feel consumed by debt. What's the worst you can imagine happening? There's no way to pay your bills??? Feel that intensely. Make it real. Now, take it further. Feel that sensation fully. Don't hold back. Continue to visualize varying levels of escalating poverty, to the point of receiving an eviction notice or seeing a foreclosure sign in the front yard, with your possessions scattered everywhere. Immerse yourself in the fear. Let it be there, soak it in totally. You may cry, sweat, or feel panicked etc. This means you are truly getting into your emotions.

See this in your mind's eye repeatedly until you've exhausted the last drop of emotion surrounding this fear. You'll find this problem doesn't carry the same weight it did before the exercise and won't consume you anymore. Now you can respond effectively instead of reacting out of fear and panic. You'll be amazed at how useful this is for working through what's scaring you.

START DOING THE OPPOSITE

The third step is to start doing the opposite of what's normal for you. There is a great *Seinfeld* episode on the WB Network where George does the opposite of what's usual and gets everything he wants. He's finally so fed up that he risks change… moving toward his fear, not away. TV education at its best, watch it and learn. Say, "yes" to life. Make changes. Go to new places and do new things. Try things you've never done. Drop the automatic barriers of "I can't," "I won't," or "I'm afraid," that say "no" to risking.

Rutgar looked up at his bookshelf and saw Feel the Fear and Do It Anyway *by Susan Jeffers. Her words influenced him to rappel off a cliff at 500 feet, get his scuba diving certificate and ask out the town's beauty queen, Missy Rochester. "That book really helps readers understand you can handle anything that comes your way," he thought to himself.*

DON'T GIVE UP ON YOURSELF

Be gentle and caring as you start this process. It's new. Let yourself make mistakes. You'll get it right. When you fall down, which we all do, pick yourself up.

75

Just keep putting one foot in front of the other. You're not alone. Don't be ashamed to ask for help. We all feel inadequate. It takes lots and lots of practice to change. The children's story about the <u>Little Engine That Could</u> was written to show this.

You are much more than you give yourself credit for. Take time to discover your fearless nature. Courage is not the absence of fear… courage develops from walking through it. John Travolta's character in the movie "Phenomena" succinctly summed it up by saying, "You have to take out your eraser and get rid of fear. It's work, hard work. And, no one can do it for you."

Suggested Starting Points For Leaving Misery Behind:

1) Build yourself up by clinging to your successes.

2) Take small steps, face fear slowly and safely.

3) Be gentle, caring and kind to yourself.

4) Talk about what frightens you. It lessens the impact.

5) Walk through threatening scenes in your head until they are boring and have no punch. Practice the exercise in the section "What's The Worst That Can Happen?" with each fear that arises. For best results do this in the moment when the feelings are the most intense.

6) Admit when you feel afraid, take a deep breath and keep walking!

Chapter 4

What's Wrong With Lying?

Do you lie? Fess up. Tell the truth, if to no one but yourself. What about the little "white" lies you consider harmless? The ones you tell to spare your feelings or someone else's. If you're one of many, let it be said in no uncertain terms that the world mirrors those lies back to you. The way you treat others is exactly how you assume they are going to treat you! It's an indisputable fact. While there may be no awareness of this consciously, on a gut level you know it. Since you do it, it must mean others do it as well. Lying is not allowed. It's dishonest and you are not here to live dishonestly. It makes everyone paranoid. Makes for uneasy feelings, squirming inside and assuming people are out to get you. Nothing else makes the world as unpredictable or untrustworthy.

Rutgar strongly agreed with what he just read. He was so satisfied with the material he pulled together on this topic that the rewrite would be a snap. There was no better word to depict the damage done by lying than **worthlessness.** *Rutgar reasoned that lying comes from feeling unworthy and naturally follows close behind Fear as Rule #4 in Misery's diabolical list of Rules & Regulations. There wasn't much to add. Feeling pleasantly surprised at his ability to assimilate information, he continued by reading out loud. Rocky watched intently waiting for a signal it was time to go out, instead Rutgar propped his feet up on the desk. He leaned back in his comfy chair and mentioned to an anticipating Rocky, "It will be your turn for a well deserved walk after listening to this masterful piece of work."*

THREE KINDS OF LYING
There are basically three kinds of lies: lying to yourself, lying to deceive, or

lying to protect, all of which begin by misleading yourself in one way or another. You must lie to yourself before you can swallow the other two. Lying occurs when people desire to defend themselves or others. It's a form of insecurity. This type of protective shield looks innocent, even helpful, but it's really just a cover-up.

Few understand that defenses only legitimize and assure the continuance of what's being run from. Unknowingly, they pay a high price for their diplomacy. False humility is slavery. It boils down to pure egotism. There's an ulterior motive. You want to be liked and approved of… that's why you lie. Fear of rejection stops you cold. You're afraid of what will happen if the truth comes out. Putting on a smile and rearranging circumstances won't rid you of the disturbing uneasiness.

A mask of self-deception is used to blanket a fear of conflict and deception's only benefit is hard knocks in the school of life. Anything gained through dishonesty or fraud subconsciously serves to remind the swindler of what's been done. Cons eventually get conned and peace is never part of the package. Results are shallow and temporary no matter how grand things appear.

"That brings to mind the time I was working on an overnight case a few years ago. We won't forget that night will we Rocky? It was getting late and we had to stay in a motel. The closest one I found did not accept pets, but I was tired and wanted to call it a night. Rather than taking into account my need to be honest, I decided I could safely get away with keeping you in the room. I convinced myself you would be quiet and staying there was not a problem. Deep down I felt bad for not telling the truth. Consequently, I tossed and turned all night afraid you'd hear a strange noise and bark. I felt rotten the next day. Besides the lack of sleep, my conscience continued nagging at me. No matter how hard I tried, I couldn't convince myself what I did was okay. We'd both have been much better off driving a bit further, finding an inn that allowed animals and getting a good night's sleep."

Whether it's someone else's hide or your own being looked after, the need to lie is strictly based in fear or inexcusable avoidance. Dishonesty via good intentions carries an air of dignity and forthrightness to the world. Look deeper. It actually characterizes the majority of lies, that's why most people feel justified telling lies to protect.

LYING IS UNDERHANDED

It's become okay to bend the truth, avoid it or make up a palatable excuse. **Everybody** does it. They're convinced it's only done "to shield" others from pain. Be nice instead of a bully, after all, nobody deserves to be hurt. Acquiesce rather than step on anyone's toes and risk embarrassment... despite the mounting animosity and hostility.

Expressing anything that might ripple the water scares the wits out of you and makes you quiver. You would rather bite your tongue than irritate a soul or tell a big fat one to defuse attention. With fierce determination you run from the one thing that will set you free: **honesty**. As Shakespeare said, "One may smile, and smile, and still be a villain."

"Rocky, that mess your dog-walker Madison got herself into was a perfect example of what happens when people think they can get away with embellishing the truth," Rutgar groaned. Rocky responded instantly to her name, eagerly looking around, swishing his tail with excitement. Madison is one of the few people Rutgar trusts Rocky with when he goes out of town.

Madison didn't feel like carrying out plans with a prospective date. Truthfully, a better opportunity came along. Instead of being straightforward and telling him she had changed her mind she decided to fib. She used the time-honored excuse that she was not feeling well. After all, it was flu season and she felt a cold coming on. Her date obligingly went along with the story. A few months later the tables were turned. Plans were set with a new fling. She looked forward to meeting him. It was exciting. Then came the call informing her the new friend wasn't feeling well. The evening was cancelled, immediately engulfing Madison in terrific self-doubt. Based on her previous actions she automatically assumed he was lying. The shoe was on the other foot now and it felt lousy.

"Lying isn't beneficial. It's underhanded and dirty. The only cure is a heavy dose of self-forgiveness and a choice to change. Madison has the opportunity to forgive another for what she did," Rutgar said to Rocky.

Relationships based on the smallest bit of deception are a farce. This theory sheds light on the growing amount of tension in society today. The term "politically correct" bears that out. Words are often deceiving, typically people say one thing and mean another. One rotten apple **can** spoil the whole barrel. It's only a matter of time. Poll the general public and ask them to respond honestly about truthful communication. The answer is not good. It's almost an oxy-moron.

THE STARTING GATE

It starts innocently. Fearing rejection or abandonment, kids want to please. It smoothes the waters and calms the storm. Since everyone knows children naturally tell the truth and call it as they see it, lying becomes a learned protective behavior. Actions leading to a negative response from parents or primary caretakers make children reconsider their options. They learn to protect themselves and others as a means of avoiding trouble, confrontation or being harmed. Wanting to live beyond adolescence, they do the "right" thing in the guise of being polite... changing their actions to suit those around them. Sadly, they learn to live through other people's opinions.

Unfortunately every episode that temporarily kept them out of trouble automatically reinforces an unnatural pattern. That precedent will continue throughout their lives. If this happened to you, be watchful of current actions. Witness the same feelings of uncertainty and emptiness coming up now that you felt then. Life has moved forward yet is anything really different?

Rutgar believes that from childhood on, trust is impossible and nothing will change that until you correct the dysfunctional lessons you learned. This means stepping up to the plate at all cost now*. Otherwise, the urge to deceive continues. Without stopping the cycle of lies you'll never experience one bit of trust.*

Living life in its purest form obliterates the need to please, eliminates having expectations, being a martyr or servitude. That pattern dissolves. You don't have to alter the facts or look for payoffs. Intimidation doesn't run you so your instincts don't pull you in that direction.

Truth always wins in the long run. The short-term advantage isn't worth the price. Everyone who cheats pays the piper. It's just a matter of "when". Your soul knows this. That's why it feels funny when you lie. In order to deceive, it's mandatory to go against your gut. A need to persuade yourself that it's okay is the first clue. Anticipation of ill-gotten gains can't override fluctuating feelings. It's wrong and you know it. That can't be said enough.

WHY NOT BE HONEST?

Truth is frightening to a lot of folks. They're afraid of being hurt. It's tough to be up-front. That's why there is little trust on a global scale. Complaints are rampant about not being able to trust "others". When all the while those feelings originate from a severe lack of trust for themselves... this lack of trust begins inside. Look at the mudslinging in politics for instance. It's not long before candidates hurl misleading rumors; then pay a publicist to counter attack. There is no integrity or dignity in this.

Rutgar deliberated the recent scandals concerning Arthur Andersen, Enron, WorldCom, Mirant, Tyco and other corporations. Each one epitomizes the toll lying takes: Fortunes destroyed, employees and stockholders betrayed, the economy damaged. All net results of individuals grossly stretching fact for profit, people who refused to tell the truth on a massive scale for the sake of personal gain, greed and the negative ego. Nobody wins. Even the ones who believe they won lose out before it's over. "It's a sad state of affairs for everyone concerned Rocky," he concluded.

These people are oblivious to how the Universal system works. Like a powerful mirror, you can bet that a similar situation will be drawn to you shortly as a reflection. It offers you an opportunity to undo the mistake you've made, to restructure your course of action. In other words, live with honor and credibility. Anything else is a waste of time.

As was stated in the beginning: If you don't trust others it's because you don't trust your own actions. Though you try to repress it your intuitive sense (inner guidance) offers sensory feedback constantly, and "others" simply reflect back what's in its way. How can you hold anyone else accountable for telling the truth when you lie? That's unrealistic. Yet surprisingly, we all do it. Whether the presenting issue acts as a reminder that you lie to other people or to yourself, it filters down to one thing... a lie is a lie. Don't take this lightly. The Universe will keep recreating these opportunities until you catch on.

BACK TO BASICS

Your sole purpose is to be who you are, without pretense or fear. That means taking the action required to face inadequacy. As an experiment, go through an entire day consciously choosing to be honest. Start by dealing with the unvarnished truth **internally**. It's not as easy as it sounds. The fear of exposure is gripping and this approach is unsettling at first. **Don't breathe a word** of what you're doing to anyone until you are stronger. Watch how awkward and uncomfortable it feels when it's time to face the music. Be aware of how quickly panic and doubt shoot through your system trying to stop you.

It's a matter of not believing you are important enough to have a voice. Speak freely, like the unexpected words of a small child, without fear. Telling it like it is, openly expressing the way you see it. You are here to be candid, frank, direct, blunt, outspoken or any other word that promotes truthfulness. Only as an adult, use compassion in your delivery. Keep in mind how you would like what you're about to say, said to you. Use tact and discretion, but find a voice. The most valued people are the ones who live this way.

"Rocky you always act out your truth whether it's barking for joy or growling at the people you don't like!"

Lying is a nasty routine that's hard to break. If you are not prepared, discovering how you maneuver in life can be startling. Being truthful may not be your highest priority. Observe yourself and see. Find out exactly where you dance around the truth. Get back to basics. Train yourself to speak honestly, no more hedging. It's scary, but frequent application lessens the hesitation. You are **okay** despite what you say, feel or do. Your feelings **can** be trusted. Express the truth compassionately, as you see it. Then pat yourself on the back.

Over time, you'll feel safer with yourself and those around you. Like that strict teacher, Mrs. Crenshaw mentioned in Chapter One, it's beneficial to reflect on the people you admire the most. The ones who made you feel uncomfortable with their directness. You always trusted them, didn't you? You knew in your heart they cared. Make a difference like those people did. Not only does it feel better, you will walk with your head held high. Relish the power, alive-ness and freedom that truth brings. Lies beget lies. Honesty begets honesty. Take your pick.

SUGGESTED STARTING POINTS For LEAVING MISERY BEHIND:

1) Be alert to the number of times you automatically want to lie or stretch the truth.

2) Investigate what you are trying to protect with a lie.

3) Who is actually being cheated or deceived?

4) Ask yourself what you are avoiding or what is motivating you not to tell the truth.

5) Look at why the consequences of a lie are scarier than the truth.

6) Examine how a lie can reap any benefit.

7) Admit the truth (even if its only to yourself at first).

8) Work toward gently and compassionately externalizing your internal truth.

Chapter 5

Defensiveness

"Do you ever find yourself feeling like one of the walking wounded? Are you overly sensitive or touchy? Do you hate being vulnerable? Are you someone who is bothered by what other people do? Do you feel like there's a chip on your shoulder the size of the Mount Everest? Then like it or not, you are defensive! If the word itself creates a little reaction, you fit the profile." Rutgar found these imposing questions earmarked in his notebook "Simple Practical Ways To Get Out of a Mess – Or Another Way To Look At Problems" while searching for the right way to explain the damage caused by taking things too personally.   Those reflective statements are strong. Nobody will miss the point. Full of excitement Rocky darted in out of nowhere and jumped on the couch, wrestling with the pillows and tossing them in the air. "Rocky, you little rascal, thanks for reminding me to keep it light."

Rutgar had to agree with Rule #5 in Misery's Welcome Kit, being defensive is like a bad sunburn. When things hit too close to home there's no mistaking the hot spots. It leaves you feeling raw, exposed and unable to budge. When anything trips your trigger you immediately recoil and withdraw. Rutgar noticed that people who get defensive are **resistant** to feedback and don't feel accepted by others or themselves. They feel numb and helpless. It shows in every aspect. Facial expressions and body language quickly report extreme sensitivity and noticeable ego inflammation. "Just like when Rocky puts his tail between his legs when he is scolded," Rutgar agreed quietly to himself.

THE LOW SELF-WORTH FACTOR

Rutgar continued wading through the pages of his notebook to rewrite Rule #5. With the exception of that one area he found right off the bat he wasn't having much luck and got discouraged. It started wearing on him. He noticed how fast emotions could flip especially when irritation is heightened. Rocky started barking at the mailman and in Rutgar's agitated state he snapped at his little buddy, who only minutes earlier he had been praising. Frustrated, Rutgar pushed away from his desk and stomped toward the kitchen. He saw his faithful friend sulking on the sofa in the library as he walked by. It caught him off guard, but then he laughed at his own behavior. He promptly went over to his trusty companion, eagerly made an effort to make up and said, "Sorry ole' boy, I guess I don't need a book to tell me about defensiveness. I seem to be very capable of it myself."

Touchiness is a blatant symptom of having little or no self-worth. Being sensitive means you judge other people's points of view as being more important than yours. You wouldn't react if you didn't. Most of the time, no matter how much you disagree inside, you invariably yield to somebody else's beliefs outside. You refuse to be seen as a peer and this is what makes you angry. Rather than being self-important and seeing yourself as an equal by calmly sharing your thoughts, you act out. Most of the time you become belligerent, quarrelsome or guarded, fueling the mounting upset. Practicing the silent treatment is a dead giveaway.

To top it off, the defensiveness openly exhibited makes it awfully difficult for anyone to honestly communicate with you. People who know you are prone to watch what they say when you're around, one slip of the tongue and you act destroyed. The flash of your eyes reassures them immediately. If looks could kill, they'd be dead. Sometimes you quickly try to lighten the air by making a comeback with witty dagger-like responses trying to impose some of the pain back on them, but it's easy for everyone to tell you are hurt by the scowl on your face. This is never fun by any stretch of the imagination and what led Ethel Barrymore to say, "You grow up the day you have the first real laugh... at yourself!"

Rutgar could see where " lying to protect " from the previous chapter readily comes into play in this scenario. Margaret, his co-chair, on the Charity Committee was truly defensive when it came to anyone judging her ideas for the annual auction. The others always trip over themselves to agree with her so that they won't hurt her feelings or risk having her lash out at them for a difference of opinion. The sad part was when she wasn't re-elected for co-chairperson this past year, she had no idea that the reason stemmed totally from her opinionated, aggressive behavior.

An additional shortfall of this less-than-attractive picture is a lack of earnestness on both sides. Because of your guarded nature, nobody is willing to be real or genuine with you. It's too uncomfortable. Why deal with it? It's not their problem. So people simply distance themselves. As a result, you intuitively feel them withholding. Everyone can attest to the lack of sincerity in the air. Nobody feels the slightest bit safe. This makes you feel even more insecure than before. You don't trust them, and they won't trust you.

THE DEFENSIVE DANCE

No one wants to live this way so how does this defensiveness dance get started in the first place? Rutgar's neighbor, Justin, hired a very meticulous contractor to renovate his home. "By all accounts, this builder is a perfectionist," he said. "Unfortunately, because this fellow schedules jobs back to back, there's no room for error, no space left to compensate for potential problems. This guy is friendly enough, but high-strung, under a lot of pressure and stressed out."

"At the end of the job we were walking through the punch-list, going over each item carefully to be sure nothing was missed when the remodeler suddenly blew up. He ranted and raved about how Justin was inferring that he was stupid, and that nothing he did was good enough. In Justin's mind, he was being considerate of the builder's time by trying to eliminate the possibility of a return visit. Justin could see it was fruitless based on the builder's highly reactionary behavior."

88

He was utterly shocked at the contractor's unexpected reaction. Justin had cleared his own emotional baggage to the point that this guy's actions did not faze him. Calmly asking the builder why he was upset, he stated that criticism had never crossed his mind and that he had done nothing but praise his work. The fellow's emotions settled down and he admitted that he was under too much pressure due to other deadlines. A heartfelt apology was offered and all ended well. Rutgar was proud of Justin's ability to respond vs. react.

Deep inside each of us there's an instinctual pull to do things the right way so we don't get into trouble. Quite early on, most of us figure out what works in our particular environments. Certain reactions elicit approval and acceptance while others evoke disapproval and disappointment. Over the years various definitions of proper and improper behavior were established. They had to be obeyed whether we liked it or not. These definitions either built us up or tore us down, maybe a little of both. Praise and approval allowed us to feel good about ourselves. The criticism or condemnation doled out did just the opposite. It made us feel unsafe and unworthy.

Since disapproval and disappointment felt crappy we did what we could to avoid them. But that didn't always work. That's where the problem began. When what we learned didn't pan out, it made us feel confused. The confusion made us feel stupid because we didn't understand how to fix what was happening. Then we judged ourselves for not understanding. It made us feel inadequate. Anger played a role too. We didn't know how to stop the cycle and before long we felt ashamed and guilty. That's how the self-protective sequence started. A full-blown case of defensiveness developed and continues to be perfected as the years pass.

WHAT ARE YOU DEFENSIVE ABOUT?

You don't have to look far. It is as obvious as the nose on your face. Judgment showing up as some form of non-acceptance is the underlying issue. Some common topics that spark immediate reaction are those involving weight, education, status, debt, looks, jobs, income-level, friends, family and close relationships. These are typical areas where you feel sensitive about not doing it right or not measuring up. Areas where a lot of maddening "if only's" run through your mind constantly.

Take Adrian for instance, a previous client of Rutgar's. A fellow who never completed his degree, which makes him feel insecure and never good enough as a result. He avoids intellectuals like the plague and works like a Trojan to prove his worth at work. His self-judgment overshadows any feelings of accomplishment. No matter how hard he tries self-doubt inevitably takes precedence over feeling successful, despite his six-figure income. To top it off, he's read enough books to fill a library and keeps up with current events in an effort to overcompensate. Nothing fills the void or the emptiness he feels for not following through. The solution to his problem is to be honest. Honest in facing the fact he feels inadequate for not graduating. Rutgar sadly shook his head and then said teasingly, "Rocky, my crafty little canine, you've got a PH.D. when it comes to confronting life."

Rutgar knows that there's nothing wrong with making that kind of decision. The real stumbling block is continued self-judgment, which fortifies your own non-acceptance. This legitimizes defenses and eliminates the prospect of change. You think you've risked accepting yourself by ignoring society's so called "rules," but it's only a slick con job. Possible solutions are intricately screened and warded off. You're too guarded to admit vulnerability about what hurts and do something about it. You'd rather remain raw.

You don't have to be run by these learned beliefs. Remember who is in charge now! It would feel a lot better if you weren't so sensitive, admitted your self-induced shortcomings and began finding solutions by fully accepting them. When you notice yourself flinching even the slightest bit it's a dead give-away your emotions are starting to flare. Don't pretend or lie to yourself about this either! You can tell when you're provoked. You wouldn't feel that sting if you weren't. Feeling a mild twinge of annoyance or the blood violently rushing through your system is a distinct clue.

IDENTIFYING EXISTING WOUNDS

Reacting is a good rule of thumb for signaling a direct hit on an existing wound. If you react, you've got something to defend. Defending means you feel guilty. Take a moment to think about it: Reacting means re-in-act. That makes it simple. When you react, you recreate the same emotions by reconstructing the event over and over in your mind. Notice any reoccurring themes? Life is full of them.

Doesn't it strike you as weird that each time you've gotten rid of one irritating idiot another one comes out of nowhere? Try comprehending this concept: All those people who get on your nerves and drive you absolutely batty will continue to do so until you figure out why they rub you the wrong way and deal with what lies behind it. Ignoring them isn't healthy or helpful. It only perpetuates a cycle of repetition and redundancy.

Need a little more proof? Would you react if someone called you a cup? No. Or would you react if someone said horrible things in a language you didn't understand? No. It's only when things are heard, accepted as being real, and carry the smallest hint of truth behind them that they bite. You'll never find yourself reacting to anything unless it's true for you on some level. Items that normally get your attention are usually the things that have a definite impact or strike a resounding note.

Being defensive doesn't protect you. It makes matters worse. That's guaranteed. You can't ignore what's bothering you. It's too difficult. It won't just disappear into thin air. Not only do the jabs continue they become increasingly sharper and more forceful. When something bumps up against you don't deny it. Own it. Painful imprints from the past seek release. They'll be permanent residents until you persistently kick them out. As a matter of fact they'll follow you everywhere you go.

STOP THE DEFENSIVE DANCE

If you are tired of the defensive two-step voluntarily investigate why you are touchy, where it stems from and how your particular brand of defensiveness began. Make a list of at least ten areas where you feel vulnerable. Call it "Areas of Vulnerability." Pinpoint high-pressure areas. Identify what makes you fly off the handle. Then write an additional list of ten items with the heading of "I Would Be Better If." Insecurities around areas where "buttons can be pushed," are identified in no time. It's not a tough assignment and won't take long. Put both lists somewhere in plain sight and frequently review them. Be honest about why these are hot spots and prepare yourself to be confronted so you can clean them out. It's one way the Universe works to help us.

Be clear as to where past actions don't match current beliefs. Rutgar chose to use the above suggestions to work through areas where he was defensive. He felt the people in Misery ought to do likewise. Make an agreement with yourself to continue this process until your inner world is as harmonious as your outer world. It can be a lot of fun. A wise sage once said, "Instead of trying to cover the world with leather, make yourself a pair of shoes and walk."

<u>Suggested Starting Points For Leaving Misery Behind</u>:

1) Pay attention to touchiness and catch yourself when you react.

2) Admit your shortcomings and be aware of when you are feeling vulnerable or sensitive.

3) If you have a need to defend yourself you must believe you've been attacked. Use insecurity, approval seeking and feelings of unworthiness as tools or clues to check problem areas.

4) Remember that an opinion is just that, an opinion, not necessarily a fact.

5) When you are hooked by another's comments or actions look for the root cause.

6) Learn to respond vs. react.

7) Write a list of vulnerable areas and work on strengthening them.

Chapter 6

Rationalize, Analyze & Stuff

Rationalizing, analyzing and stuffing… now there's a destructive combination! The first two don't seem bad. They're supposed to help you do some well-intentioned soul searching and appear to be great problem solving techniques… until it comes to emotions. In that instance both are ingenious ways to accomplish the third, which is to stuff feelings.

Rutgar knew the result of stuffing your feelings…. it's like overindulging on Thanksgiving Day. You get to the point where you've crammed down so much food you're numb, unfeeling and unable to move… **anesthetized** *by all the stuffing you've been doing. Rutgar felt that word drove the point home and succinctly described the cumulative effects of Rationalizing, Analyzing and Stuffing for his rewrite of Rule #6.*

Each of these nasty traits forms a unique intellectual stumbling block. This is guaranteed to keep you actively in your head, far away from the truth of your emotions and deceptively detoured from feeling what's happening to you. Some people are proud of this ability. Frankly it's a curse. As John Dewey said, "Anyone who has begun to think places some portion of the world in jeopardy." It's nothing to be excited about and anything but helpful for a peaceful life. The need to rationalize or analyze is a slick way to deflect dealing with things that bother you. Feelings rising to the surface are stuffed so quickly by thinking that you're seldom aware of doing it.

THE ROOT OF RATIONALIZATION

The main reason you dive headfirst into rationalization is because at some point a feeling knocked up against you that was uncomfortable or unacceptable. You didn't like it or know what to do with it so it became something to be avoided. Things didn't quite fit the picture you had painted for yourself. Instead of mounting a frontal attack by facing your feelings you ingeniously decided to skate around the issue bypassing the entire situation. You regrouped by plunging into the thinking process… or so you believed. Plainly put, you thought instead of felt.

The habit of skillfully rationalizing attempts to ward off self-confrontation. Justifying every possible reason why what you felt is wrong, crazy, troublesome or untimely; you devalue and bully yourself into accepting an outcome that isn't okay and doesn't feel right in the first place. You pretend everything is all right even though you feel yucky on the inside. Despite feeling thrown you fake a contented look and move forward. It's unsettling. You trick yourself into believing it's gone, and worst of all, **you** do this to **you**. Why? The obvious answer is to get rid of it. Surprise! The feeling hasn't gone anywhere and it will resurface when you least expect it… probably at a very inconvenient time.

The habit of analyzing compounds the problem. That murky feeling in your gut demands you dissect every little thing, scrutinizing each detail, staying totally focused on the problem. This blocks the possibility of any hint of emotion sneaking in. Analyzing obstructs feelings. Thinking and feeling cannot exist simultaneously. It prevents feelings from surfacing in a spontaneous, child-like way like they ought to. "Out of sight, out of mind." Not out of touch though. That's why analyzers feel repressed and become walking time bombs.

Rutgar's mind drifted back to when his best friend Sid, lost his father. He didn't want to deal with the grief that seemed all consuming. Instead he dove into making the funeral arrangements and caring for the visiting mourners. He felt they needed his comfort more than he needed theirs. Rutgar offered to leave Rocky with him to keep him company but Sid said he was fine. The next week, Sid and Rutgar went out to dinner. When Sid's food came, the whole order was messed up. Normally, an easy-going guy, Sid made a scene yelling very loudly at the waitress. He ended up in tears at the table sobbing uncontrollably. His grief won out.

UNSTUFF - FEEL INSTEAD OF THINK

Thinking isn't feeling and feeling is an important tool in life. Thinking is stuffing, not experiencing or savoring feelings in the moment - **both** positive and negative feelings. Feelings separate us from computers, without them you are nothing more than a robot. When you use mental software to decipher what is happening emotionally or pick things apart in minute detail you lock-up. Eventually you have to reboot. It won't work long term. It can't. It's ineffectual.

When operating correctly feelings act as indicators or alarms that something is being set off inside. When it's time to act they scream out, but all too often you don't listen to them. You've inadvertently trained yourself to follow your intellect instead of addressing feelings.

Turning away from unwanted feelings has a major impact... it gives them increased power, strength and importance. Resistance builds momentum. It has to. They demand attention and like water behind a dam, blocked feelings build up force daily. The underlying tension will grab hold of you eventually. Pretending a bomb isn't there won't stop it from exploding. Feelings are no different, as Sid's story proves.

Look at this from a little different angle. If you don't like spiders because they terrify you no amount of intellectual convincing is going to change your mind and make them cute. Even if a person who loves spiders spends untold hours telling you about their magnificent contribution to the environment, it's doubtful your feelings about spiders are going to change any time soon. You might learn to tolerate them, but will you ever appreciate them? Test it. Let a big furry one crawl on your face or arm and see if the pep talk worked.

Rationalizing, analyzing or stuffing are all non-emotional and only **appear** to be viable ways to escape uncomfortable feelings. If you knew of the far-reaching consequences you'd quit. They deceptively furnish convenient explanations to convince you action has been taken, when what you've actually done is slip around the real issue... the natural process of needing to feel. It's a paradox. Allowing feelings to be there ironically makes them dissolve and disappear. It's that simple. "Jump in and swim."

Thinking about the people in Misery made Rutgar shake his head as he took a break from writing. He started to talk to Rocky about what he was thinking, but quickly stopped because his cherished buddy was napping contentedly. He figured Misery's residents would ridicule his version of the Kit as being repetitive and wanted to share that with Rocky as he mulled it over. "What better excuse to avert change?" He whispered, and then went back to writing. Nothing was going to stop him. Even if only one person caught his message the whole project was worth his time and effort. He was certain they would eventually discover each chapter is poignant at various stages in life. While seemingly similar, each chapter has unique characteristics distinctly setting it apart from the others.

ACKNOWLEDGE THERE'S AN ISSUE

Intellectually trying to manage sidestepped feelings kids you into believing you are a strong person. To dismiss what's stuck emotionally is not that simple. To assure distance you logically and methodically compartmentalize concerns convinced you've gotten rid of them. This action only serves to make you feel strung out and exhausted from lugging around the additional emotional baggage you've skillfully avoided.

Rutgar knew most of his clients were infected with the current rationalizing, analyzing and stuffing epidemic and wondered who else was ailing. "They'll know if they never sit still, work incessantly and make unending lists. Add to that those who cannot sleep, read voraciously and are non-stop thinkers because they are riddled with anxiety. Let's not forget the ones who cry easily or can only tear up watching movies and commercials. Don't they realize feelings don't go away and internal pressure is weighing them down from the heavy load they're carrying? Like a good wine that's been on the shelf too long, they ferment and sour."

No amount of self-talk is going to change what's eating at you. If a spider caught you off guard you'd scream bloody murder, feel scared and squish the poor spider to smithereens… despite those lengthy lectures you heard about how great they were. You don't like those suckers, period.   Be realistic about how you feel. Facing issues squarely is safer and dissolves distasteful consequences.

Experiencing a "light bulb" moment Rutgar picked up his precious pooch and swung him around. Rocky started barking not understanding his owner's exuberance. "Rocky, my dear fellow, it's become so clear how these three fit. Rationalizing, analyzing and stuffing remind me of the times you guard a precious bone… nothing is coming near that prized possession. Then you bury it, the same way the people in Misery use their minds to keep emotions from surfacing and stuff them away. There's no benefit. You can't enjoy your bone and they can't enjoy life. Both of you are always on guard. Creativity at its height!"

BREAK THE HABIT

Don't be too hard on yourself if this is a habit of yours. The whole analyzing process is automatic. You don't even realize you do it. It's picked up along the way to allow you to deal with things you don't understand. It acts as a legitimate intellectual barrier created to help you manage situations that seem out of your control. Thinking offers a much-needed pause, creating distance from what upsets you.

Initially going into your head offered an escape that helped, but it's not good to make a steady diet of it. The analytical process fills a need. Understanding the how's and why's is helpful, but when it's perpetual, it's a tradition you want to break. Maneuvering and manipulating emotions is a temporary fix at best. Familiar situations that show up frequently, shaded with remnants of the past, are a slap in the face to help you wake up. Steering clear of feelings rather than meeting them head on, is what creates problems. Where on earth do you think these feelings go? You can't possibly believe that if you wait long enough they'll mystically disappear. Can you?

100

One of Rutgar's astute teachers posed that question years ago, then explained what happens: "Be forewarned anything not dealt with or left unfinished from a prior experience must be worked through or it's going to keep resurfacing. **Stuck feelings are relentless.** *No matter how hard you try to think them away... they want to be felt... and* **will be felt** *one way or the other. You can't hold them at bay forever. Be prepared for lots of return visits. That is where patterns come from... emotions wanting attention, hanging around to be dealt with and freed up." She concluded with a wry grin on her face saying, "Why not save some time and simply get it over with?"*

Pain hurts and no amount of "understanding" why it hurts will remove it. You can't think away pain. Pain only dissolves by allowing it. Sit in it. That means feeling the feelings you are running from completely, not repressing or turning them away. It's like you are coated in mud and badly in need of a bath. Feel them to the max (like the example in Chapter #3) no matter how scary or ugly they appear. What a great way to face your emotional junk such as hurt, rejection, resentment or anything else that arises right there on the spot. Look into it, feel it and admit your shortcomings.

Develop a plan of action. If you are going to use the mind use it constructively to become more aware of, and walk through, distorted beliefs. Open up to discomfort and welcome what you don't like. It's your own stuff you are up against. It may not feel good, but it is a necessary part of life. Express the truth to yourself then, if appropriate, to others when you're ready.

"Rocky, we're half way through the rewriting of Misery's Rules & Regulations and the connection is unmistakable. Not being Selfish with a Capital "S" leads to Avoiding and Pretending. Avoiding and Pretending leads to Fear. Fear leads to Lying. Lying leads to Defensiveness and Defensiveness leads to Rationalizing, Analyzing and Stuffing. Going backward or forward it's mind-blowing to witness how these emotion-twisters devour a person's sanity." Rocky was still napping and didn't flinch.

HIT THE BRAKES

If your natural reaction is to "think" first and feel second (or not at all), give it a rest. Instantly ask yourself how you "feel" instead. Get in touch with what is going on inside your body and in your heart. With a little effort, it's not hard to discover what's happening inside. Ask yourself at least one hundred times a day, "How am I feeling?" That's simple enough and eliminates emotional cover-ups. This means **feel**, **feel**, **feel**, and **feel** some more. Don't allow yourself to justify anything. Don't allow yourself to excuse anything away. Don't allow yourself to defend anything. Don't allow yourself to put up with anything that's not okay with you.

Disconcerting situations don't happen by accident. They do have a purpose! This purpose is to make you feel your feelings. Unexpected devices of all kinds are sent to make you realize this, but whenever you rationalize, analyze or stuff you kill the messenger. Stop reverting into your head to steer feelings away. **If you miss this point things are apt to get worse.**

The world you live in runs smoothly on its own if you pay attention. **"Feel your feelings"** can't be emphasized enough. They are truly a gift. Respect them, honor them and appreciate them, otherwise it's like running into a hornet's nest and trying to figure out why the painful bites sting. It hurts because it hurts… period. You don't think about it when you're injured, do you? You say ouch! As author Jerry Jampolsky, M.D. aptly said about the intellect, "The longest journey you will ever take is the eighteen inches from your head to your heart."

SUGGESTED STARTING POINTS FOR LEAVING MISERY BEHIND:

1) The number one rule is to "feel your feelings" first, then decide what to do.

2) Practice the "Learn to Live in the Now" exercise in Chapter #3.

3) Act like a child – simply be in the moment with whatever is happening.

4) Don't project into the future or revert to the past.

5) Stop outlining, plotting and planning.

6) Stay absolutely right now!

Chapter 7

Point One Finger Out
(Ignore The Three Pointing Back)

*Rutgar dreaded reviewing this chapter. He knows that finger pointers are terminally dependent on blame. They want to escape from their own reality instead of confronting what's truly bothering them. They are convinced pointing a finger shields them from dealing with what they are desperately trying to escape. These people are exceptionally talented; having already mastered the other six topics covered in Misery's Welcome Kit and they are now ready to move on to **projecting** their problems outside, finding others to attack. "What a fitting word to categorize this rewrite of Rule #7," Rutgar scoffed. In his line of work this underlies 80% of his cases. The number of new files opened by clients determined to find fault with someone else is mind-blowing.*

Rutgar felt cynically amused. He knows it doesn't work. Blaming others is a temporary fix. Pointing a finger seems like a short cut, a clever distraction to avert ownership. It's not, no matter how justified your plight seems to be. Instead of offering freedom, projection creates a constant reflection of your denial. What you avoid internally ends up driving you and controlling your actions just like MicroSoft software runs most computers. Daily, these repressed emotions affect everything that crosses your path. You wouldn't be pulling out that finger unless something is getting a little too close for comfort. It doesn't matter if predicaments are large or small; the bottom line is something is eating away at you.

Projection means, "to throw out or hurl away from or toward something else."

104

It's a sneaky way to circumvent ownership of trouble, redirecting responsibility outside yourself and leaving it there. "Scapegoat" accurately describes this function.

Rutgar read that the word "scapegoat" originally comes from an ancient Judaic custom. Once a year, the people of the village brought a goat into camp, cast their sins upon the animal and then ran it out of town. "It wasn't hard to see from the moral of the story," he snickered whimsically "how projecting is an easy way to unload what is threatening or frightening." About that time Rocky wanted attention, but Rutgar wouldn't give him the time of day. Rocky wouldn't give up and overtly jumped toward the desk hitting Rutgar's arm, knocking the notebook to the floor. Rutgar was missing Rocky's point. This incident ticked Rutgar off and in his agitated state he scolded Rocky for his behavior. He had ignored Rocky's determination to be noticed, projecting his irritation instead. As fate would have it the notebook opened to this.

THE OTHER GUY IS NOT YOUR PROBLEM

The age-old saying, "One finger out means three pointing back" is poignant and filled with truth and wisdom. As a matter of fact, just hearing these words ignites fury and intense irritation in many folks. Say it to someone who is attacking you and watch what happens! It makes them fuming mad or uneasy, to say the least. Shuts them up pretty fast to boot. Immediately disagreeing, these people are quick to fire back that the whole concept is sheer and utter nonsense.

Whenever people find themselves reacting to that saying there's an acknowledgement of some kind going on deep inside; an inadvertent awareness that their finger pointing out means they are actually talking about themselves. When that's recognized they don't like it. Nobody gets upset about anything unless it strikes up against something personal. That's the reason finger pointing was created. It's a reaction to buttons being pushed and serves as a handy tool for taking a defensive stance.

Why? Nobody would react or be defensive unless the words hit too close to home, especially with regard to the three fingers pointing back. Truthfully, it's never the other guy who is the problem. As Alexander Pope aptly put it, "All looks yellow to a jaundiced eye."

Rutgar breathed a heavy sigh. This type of client always calls to tattle on another person. He generally went through the motions of researching the situation but when all was said and done, ended up confronting the client who initiated the case. They didn't like it but each and every time they saw it was their own actions that needed to be reviewed and worked on. This was when he reiterated the point that "he/she" attracted the situation somehow and all parties played a part. "Rocky could have handled these cases for me," he grumbled. They were easily "sniffed" out.

YOU'RE NOT A VICTIM

When you point a finger at someone else, you blame. You relegate control of your life to something outside of you, which makes you a victim, and you are not here to be a victim. Finger pointers refuse to turn inward and have a relationship with themselves deflecting responsibility like the plague. They don't realize irritating people are a grit of sand that forms a pearl.

Rutgar sarcastically teased Rocky in the same condescending tone he usually heard from clients, "Look at what he/she did... If they would only... I can't stand it when... Can you believe? You know Rocky, these statements or anything similar deny you have power and authority of your own. Your quality of life is then dependent on things that are external to you. It's a great way to alleviate taking ownership for your own 'stuff'. The undeniable truth is that no one is ever responsible for another. No one can do anything to anybody without permission. This is a heavy-duty realization that is imperative."

Whatever emotional damage is done, we do to ourselves. Each individual chooses to give particular words or actions power according to his respective perception. "It's like each one of us is encased in an acrylic bubble. I can't get into your bubble and you can't get into mine. Whatever I project out stays in my bubble and isn't going anywhere until I clean it out. Others merely knock up against the gunk already floating around in our bubbles." *Rutgar had jotted down those important words because they had such a great impact… time and again he'd watched them play out in his life and the lives of others.*

IRRITATIONS SERVE A PURPOSE

Everything, and that means **everything**, that makes your blood pressure rise is there to support you in dissolving judgments of some sort. The Universe wants you to be free. Like storm-driven waves against the sand, anything blocking the natural flow of life pounds up against you until rendered powerless. That's why nuisances are in your life. They show up to illuminate areas that need attention and are there to teach you, not to antagonize you. When investigated they end up lightening your load, even though it doesn't look that way in the beginning.

How does this concept work? We know the person pointing the finger is agitated or shaken. Size or significance as to why doesn't matter. This first point is probably the most familiar when defining the concept of one finger out three pointing back. There are also two less known conditions that arise for the person the finger is aimed at.

The first one will find, you, the finger pointer, a **catalyst** for the person at the end of your finger. Not only have you unearthed a touchy area in your life, at the same time you've uncovered a sensitive subject for him. You've set him off by stirring up something he doesn't want to deal with either. On some level what you represent is punching his buttons just as he is punching yours. Any reaction lets him know you've done him a favor. You both win! You've clearly shown he has work to do as well or he wouldn't react, would he?

The second of the two conditions is equally as important to understand. If any of the words spoken by the offending finger pointer knock up against you (in any form or fashion), even though that person is ultimately talking about himself; then this particular problem is yours also. You'll know if something is your issue if you find yourself being **hooked** within ten seconds. Whether you feel a mild twinge of annoyance, a subtle pull of emotion or strong jab... if you care about yourself, you'll get busy discovering why.

Thus the saying, "What you see, you be." How can another's words grab your attention or do damage if they don't have power? If they weren't significant they would simply go in one ear and out the other without notice.

You are intelligent, so you'll want to have a working knowledge of these three distinct aspects of finger pointing: 1) Blaming others, 2) Accepting blame, and 3) Being hooked by the words of others. Each offers tremendous insight, as well as a powerful jump-start toward personal growth and self-confidence. Whenever you discover a hot spot about **anything**... delve into it. Ask yourself why this thing that's bugging you annoys you at all. It's either reminding you of something you've done in the past and haven't let go of yet or it's knocking up against something you want to do (but won't give yourself permission). Go inside. Take a quick emotional inventory of what hidden judgment needs to be dissolved.

Rutgar decided the following illustrations about a few of his neighbors offered some sorely needed assistance: Lets say that once upon a time you cheated on your significant other like Nicole did. Now she's dating this really, really great guy. He has a female friend, a buddy, but no matter how much he reassures Nicole they are just friends she never feels trusting. Deep down inside she's afraid his friend will have ulterior motives and do what she did. That's because she is still feeling guilty about her past actions.

These feelings let her know that she hasn't forgiven herself. She needs to work on thoroughly letting this mistake go internally, so she is free to move on to a meaningful relationship without the fear, guilt or doubt. Backtracking through your own past is the fastest and most efficient way to guarantee clear understanding of anything that trips emotional triggers. It guarantees freedom too.

Next there was Mitch, a guy whose father traveled all the time. He grew up feeling abandoned and alone because he didn't receive the attention he desired from his dad. As an adult he tends to be touchy and sorely disappointed when occasionally his girlfriend has to work late or go out of town. He takes it personally. He ends up verbally attacking her because he feels alienated. They end up in a huge fight when normally they are a content couple.

If Mitch would remember the three fingers staring back at him he could easily identify the root of his problem. It isn't about her, but about his unresolved pain. Simply by asking questions like, "When have I felt like this before" or "What is this situation trying to tell me" answers begin to surface and you're headed in the right direction.

Sandra, another of Rutgar's neighbors, grew up with a critical father. According to him nothing she did was good enough. Consequently she's always felt worthless and had problems with intimacy. As an adult she finds the guys she's attracted to become condescending and critical as the relationship develops. She retaliates by pointing her finger at the men she dates, constantly reassuring herself that each one has a gigantic problem with self-esteem and takes it out on her.

Sandra doesn't seem to catch the fact she's the one attracting them, or that in actuality, her relationships have created exactly the same feelings she experienced growing up. She rationalizes her predicaments by blaming rather than doing a "U" turn and turning within. Ultimate solutions are found by going inside. Why? It's NEVER the other guy who is the problem.

U-TURNS

From now on take a piercing look inside before you point that loaded finger out. Remember there are always three fingers pointing back. What's important to notice is that **something** caught your attention, no matter what the issue seems to

109

be. The other person is never your problem... ever! And, no amount of justifying will change that fact.

As long as anything bugs you, rest assured you've got work to do. Here's the acid test of accomplishment: a problem is totally gone when the issue no longer presents itself in your life or doesn't create a reactive response. There's no reaction because there is nothing left inside. You won't be pointing fingers because the interior of your house is spotlessly clean. The following sums it up well:

THE TWO WOLVES – AUTHOR UNKNOWN

One evening an old Cherokee was teaching his grandchildren about life. He noticed that one child had a terrible fight going on inside. He said, "My son, the battle within is between two wolves. One wolf represents evil: anger, fear, envy, sorrow, regret, greed, arrogance, self-pity, guilt, resentment, inferiority, lies, false pride, superiority and ego. The other stands for good: joy, peace, love, hope, sharing, friendship, serenity, humility, kindness, empathy, benevolence, generosity, truth, compassion and faith. The same fight going on inside you is going on inside every other person too." The grandson thought about it for a minute then asked his grandfather, "Which wolf wins?" The old Cherokee simply replied, "The one you feed."

SUGGESTED STARTING POINTS FOR LEAVING MISERY BEHIND:
1) Be on guard for emotional trigger points.
2) Think before you speak.
3) Make a "U" turn inside before accusing anyone.
4) Take responsibility for how you feel.
5) Look at yourself before you criticize, condemn or find fault.
6) Be honest about trying to deflect situations or side step the truth.

Chapter 8

Manipulation

Rutgar and Rocky visited a sanitarium called Whitfield Estates to do research for a case. Walking through the wards with the director they came across a room where the patient was loudly moaning, groaning and wailing. Curious, Rutgar asked the director why the man was so upset. He answered, "Why, he's suffering from unrequited love. Trying to be the perfect partner he sold his soul doing everything she wanted and giving her everything she desired. Unfortunately another man snuck in and undermined his best-laid plans, one-upping what he had done. The woman ended up choosing the second man. He couldn't deal with the rejection, went insane and this is how he handles it." Continuing down the hall they peered into a different room where another patient was beating his head against a brick wall. Surprised Rutgar asked what happened to make this guy painfully destructive. The director said rather humorously, "He got that woman." Rutgar looked down at Rocky with a big grin and said, "Lucky for you relationships aren't a problem." Rocky proudly ran in circles.

Whether it's overt or inconspicuously subtle, manipulation never pans out. It is a modified version of **dishonesty**, representative of deceit and underhanded scheming to get something. Rutgar couldn't imagine a finer term to characterize his re-draft of Misery's Rule #8. Sly and devious sum it up. "If that's what you resort to, to get what you want, you are in big trouble."

MANIPULATION AS A TOOL

Those that use manipulation as a tool have piled so many layers on top of their true feelings they've forgotten how to respect them. The reality of a situation isn't providing the desired outcome, so they fall back on manipulation as a means to an end or allow themselves to be manipulated. Either way, the truth isn't suitable and "taking things into your own hands" seems to be more satisfactory. You want to be in charge.

Suffice it to say the need to manipulate is not healthy. A fatal flaw is the notion it's required to discard unwanted feelings. Feelings don't disappear via mental gymnastics. The fact that manipulation plays the smallest part at all proves you are headed in the wrong direction, certain to end up experiencing unwanted results. Though some reasons may seem saintly, good intentions are not enough.

MANIPULATION = FALSE HOPE

Manipulation offers a false sense of **hope**. But that false sense of **hope** never delivers. It's like taking a drug to ward off dissatisfaction. It offers the premise that if you can at least look forward to what you want and work the situation to your benefit, you will eventually be happy. **Hope** forever promises a better tomorrow, acting as a sedative for feeling discontented in the now. To the addict, it makes things tolerable.

Calculated thinking provides evidence that there's an underlying motive. Spontaneity is non-existent. That's what lets you know there is a problem. But you deceive yourself, determined to show there's a method to your madness. The problem is that more and more manipulation is necessary to deal with the growing disappointment spawned from these undelivered promises. Dishonesty ends up regulating your life. Like a drug addict, you continually have to feed the habit and the vicious cycle never ends.

Clinging to the false sense of a better tomorrow is the only way you can remain where you are. Trying to override the fear of not knowing the future, you desperately strive to attain what **you** believe is good. You assume your strategy will be fulfilling, but your solution is only as strong as its foundation, which is pretty shaky.

113

People don't understand that it's the deviousness behind "trying to figure it out" and the "determination to have it your way" which is causing the damage. That's illogical, if not crazy, right? You generally find something you think will bring you happiness then destroy yourself... and sometimes others... in the process of reaching your goal.

Rutgar was well aware that relationships are traditionally a breeding ground for manipulation and knew about a great example of self-manipulation through a colleague of his. Sean's girlfriend, Heather, was frequently distant. In order to remain in the relationship with her, Sean continually had to manipulate his feelings. One technique he used was setting up situations to impress her. He forever talked himself into believing things were okay when they weren't, making excuses galore for everything that didn't feel right to him... and there were lots of things that didn't feel right. One time he even used reverse psychology threatening to leave, secretly hoping Heather would rush to him out of fear. He reasoned that if he just hung in there a little longer everything would change for the better. Ultimately the relationship fell apart. Sean felt devastated and wondered why things didn't pan out. Obviously false hope and pretense didn't alter the truth.

MANIPULATION IS DISHONEST

Having a motive or manipulating is dishonest, cheap and slimy. You don't believe you are capable of having what you want without giving something up, demanding, threatening or leaving. You arrogantly think you know what's best assuming that things working out in your favor benefit everyone concerned. In each case you will suffer. Manipulation is coming through the back door. If you do manage to get what you want you came by it underhandedly and the situation itself is a constant reminder.

When you have a motive or feel the need to manipulate, deep down you are convinced everyone else is doing it too. You never feel safe or fully trust anybody. Though your motivation may not be obvious or intentional, a motive is a motive. This is why in today's world people feel like everybody is out to get them. There is not enough honesty, too much manipulation and too many motives floating around. Think

114

of all the lost souls, hungry to feel better. If they sincerely felt deserving they wouldn't have to beg, borrow or steal to get what they want. True happiness doesn't manifest through manipulation or motive, it happens effortlessly.

Life naturally has its own unforced orderly direction. What's contrived isn't natural and what is natural isn't contrived... even though it's difficult to have staying power in today's world of faster, bigger and better being the "norm". Author Arnold Patent said it best, "If you have to struggle or effort for anything, you are going against the Universe." But you want results now, and you want life to go your way.

The real concern is that you don't know how to pay attention to your motiveless gut, which provides heartfelt intuitive answers. You choose to listen to the negative ego instead. If you cut out the negative ego a sense of calmness exists when genuine gut-level guidance flows through. Those answers are always truthful, full of integrity and for the highest good of all concerned. In the end everybody benefits. That is how you know you've tuned in and received an answer. You may feel a bit unsure, but there's no doubt the decision is correct.

*Rutgar watched Rocky slowly approach a new neighborhood dog as they took their evening walk. He cautiously sniffed the dog, checking things out a little further, **before** he risked playfully tugging at the other dog's ear. It dawned on him that if the people in Misery followed their instincts like Rocky did instead of their negative egos, they would be happy. They'd have a chance at developing the courage to leave Misery for good. "You know Rocky, it strikes me that people would be better off if they were more like dogs." Rocky's tail wagged. He liked being praised.*

THE COST OF CHANGE

The negative ego enjoys routine. It doesn't like new things. Actually, it's afraid of them. It uses manipulation and motive as cunning devices to rebuff fear. People who manipulate denounce what is stirring inside. They don't want their world rocked. They want the familiar, the known, and the expected. By inventing excuses and juggling their emotions they believe change can be averted. They can endure. They don't want to face what's being churned up.

Change might lead to opening Pandora's box, which means having to face those menacing whispers reminding them they can't do anything right, are undeserving, unimportant or not good enough. Not to mention the possibility of uncovering what's buried underneath years of neglected emotions.

Take Shelley for instance. She's been in the same job for the last 10 years. She's comfortable being in sales but doesn't like where she works. Every night while driving home she dreams about quitting and looking for a new position. The thought gives her nightmares, yet at the same time offers a challenge. She's worried that other corporations won't hire her. She was fired for being irresponsible from several jobs in her mid-twenties and rationalizes that working for this objectionable corporation is the price she has to pay for her earlier behavior. She also feels she "owes" them for keeping her employed and allowing her to work her way "up" to Account Manager. She plays the lotto often, hoping by some miracle things will change.

Rutgar was keenly aware of how Shelley's story highlighted the negative effects of manipulation: dancing around issues, accepting suffering as your lot in life and justifying your predicament. His exceptional notebook mentioned that somewhere.

Manipulation and motive give the appearance of being useful tools, but they only feed problems. As time passes irritation builds. Subconsciously, every time the situation comes to mind surrounding your lover, parent, boss or whoever the culprit is, you are reminded of the hard work it takes to stay there. Not to mention what you have to sacrifice and the pent-up frustration caused from what you forfeit… it's hard to bear.

116

If you are a parent you know that kids are notoriously good manipulators. Rutgar's nephew, Andy, is a teenager who typically succumbs to peer pressure. Recently he knew about an upcoming Friday night concert well in advance. He waited until that afternoon to ask his mom if he could borrow the car and take his friends to the event. When questioned if he had completed all of his schoolwork he admitted he still had "a little reading left to do," but would have it done by Saturday. His mom agreed to let him go. Andy told his friends he would be driving and gave them the green light to make arrangements accordingly.

Andy failed to mention to his mom that his father was very explicit about all his schoolwork being completed before he could go. When his father came home from work and discovered that Andy had gotten the okay from his mom Andy's dad told him he couldn't go. Andy countered that at this point his friends had made arrangements based on his driving. "We already bought our tickets," he argued. "Now I have to take them. Their parents made other plans and everyone is depending on me to keep my promise." Andy cleverly manipulated the situation so it was difficult for his dad to say no.

GIVE FREELY

Motives, no matter how lofty, create restrained bitterness. They are nothing but dolled-up expectation. *For instance, Rutgar's travel agent Marty told him of a couple, Marsha and Greg Smith, who booked a vacation cruise. They wanted a free upgrade to a suite but Marty told them he didn't know if that was possible. He was only allowed to give out a limited number per trip and only had one left. The following week the couple mailed Marty fifty-yard line tickets to the football game. The tickets were inside of a thank you note expressing their gratitude for helping them with their travel arrangements. He didn't think much of it until Greg called asking him how the game was and how the upgrade was coming. Greg was beside himself when Marty told him he'd given it to another couple since they seemed to be more financially strapped than the Smiths.*

Having no expectations means giving freely, without strings, and leaves no hope for a return. Nobody keeps score. If you keep track you'd better take a closer look at your actions. You are "giving to get" and an earnest inspection will reveal that you feel let down and disappointed if there is no return. There's definitely a motive or there wouldn't be a reaction. Find out why discontent reared its ugly head and use the above story as a fundamental tool in your ongoing investigation of self-discovery.

Does this mean you can't set goals or plan for the future, that you can't desire or want anything? No, certainly not. You are entitled to personal preference. But, preferences are preferences, not absolutes or something that has to be manipulated or coerced into being. When choices are truly preferences they won't cause strong reactions and you won't find yourself feeling disgruntled or angry if things don't work out.

Rutgar often reminded his clients that seeking out hordes of people who would listen to their plight, persistent self-talk or heavy doses of convincing unquestionably indicate that manipulation is present. That spells trouble!

GIVE IT UP

Practice being tolerant and have patience. Let go of motives, don't manipulate, and trust. Allow the purity of desire to be present **without** trying to figure out how it's going to appear or what you need to do to work it out. For support, reflect often on the phrase "A watched pot never boils". Stop wanting it your way by trying to influence or design a specific outcome. Let it land gently like a butterfly. When an idea prompts you to move act on it without force and spontaneously do what comes to you to do in the moment staying as **now** as possible.

Manipulation and motive destroy the present moment, destroy creativity and block manifestation. Simply acknowledge the idea's presence and leave it alone. Don't strive, push or outline. Then watch what happens. (If you lack willpower, think back on the things you've desired that held little importance to you… and how fast they showed up. There's bunches of them.) As Pope Gregory I said, "If the work of the Infinite Invisible could be comprehended by reason, it would be no longer wonderful (580 A.D.)." Too simple huh?

The amount of real power you possess is in direct proportion to the unshakeable belief you have in who you are. Truly powerful people have a noticeable sense of authority. Confidence surrounds them. You can sense that when they enter a room and you feel lighter just being around them. They are genuine, honest and real by nature. That's what produces comfort, familiarity and approachability in their company.

Choose to be one of them. Risking change can't be worse than settling. There is no excuse for making other people your answer or your problem – ever. Don't play that game. Nobody likes being railroaded. Be alert, notice the instant situations feel contrived, artificial or manufactured. It's a red flag... you wouldn't notice otherwise. It's not worth the price. Benjamin Franklin once said, "He who forsakes essential liberty for temporary safety, deserves neither liberty or safety."

Suggested Starting Points For Leaving Misery Behind:

1) Never apply pressure to yourself or another.
2) Don't play games.
3) Exerting influence in a decision indicates trouble.
4) Let go of control. A need for power means there are problems.
5) Allow things to happen instead of trying to make them happen.
6) Don't assume you know the answer or what is best.

Chapter 9

Guilt

Rutgar was very familiar with guilt. He couldn't count the number of times he went through horrendous bouts of it over Rocky. Whether it concerned taking him for a walk when he didn't feel like it, leaving him with a pet-sitter or times when he couldn't give Rocky the attention he deserved. Occasionally the pressure he felt from heavy-duty obligation to his beloved companion was staggering and he hated feeling that way.

*He could provide volumes from his own experience for rewriting #9 of Misery's Welcome Kit and whole-heartedly agreed with what one of his influential instructors taught him, that **repressed anger** provided the most appropriate description of what guilt was all about. The intuitive instructor explained it this way:*

Everybody has felt guilty at one time or another. Guilt arises when you set aside your feelings for another, not acknowledging your truth and acting on it. By refusing to tell it like it is and swallowing personal pride you take a back seat. Real feelings are stuffed in the guise of protecting another. You prefer being seen as "good," instead of being truthful. Not wanting to make waves an inner code of ethics comes into play that dictates, "I'll sacrifice me for you."

Giving up on yourself makes you feel angry. Unwritten rules teach you to repress arising anger and train you to believe it's not valid. This invalidated anger turns into feelings of guilt. Whether self-inflicted or brainwashed through conditioning, you do not believe **your** feelings are okay and the resulting emotions are hard to cope with. Some examples that spark those emotions are: being upset about toothpaste left in the sink, clothes lying on the floor, eating or drinking too much, breaking promises, taking a long lunch, flirting or skipping out on a social event. Guilt arises from ingrained "should's" or "have to's" around various kinds of behavior.

You try to gloss it over by rationalizing that what's bothering you is trivial, irrelevant or unimportant. You're certain it's not an issue but at the same time you want to get rid of these feelings as soon as possible... stuffing them quickly. They feel dirty, but glossing over an issue doesn't make it go away, it intensifies adding to the frustration. It's like having a splinter in your finger that's left unattended for too long, the pain increases, the sore swells and becomes infected.

GUILT IS NASTY

Guilt is nasty, subtle and understated. It ensnares the unwary... occurring when things that irritate or brew discomfort are brushed aside, ignored or repressed.

Rutgar could list the million and one things that his friend Katie often mentioned she felt guilty about... taking a mental health day, feeling she ought to buy a present, going out when she's wasn't in the mood or feeling like she had to be nice when she didn't want to. There were other times she felt compelled to listen to a friend or child when there were a thousand things running through her mind. She even impulsively bent the rules once, but felt shame to no end. "You know Rocky, any way you cut it fear of acting inappropriately clouds the issue. You hang your head and act sheepish when you think you've done something wrong. I wonder if dogs feel guilt like people do?"

Guilt is also a sneaky underhanded way to hide emotions, the ones you don't want to deal with openly. You slip them into an invisible box and they're secretly stored in your mental attic... hoping if you ignore them they'll go away. You scam yourself into believing they'll be forgotten over time and the residual self-condemnation from unacknowledged feelings quietly slips unnoticed into the background.

Self-worth diminishes as a result of this avoidance. Deserve-ability is on the way out too. There's a high price to pay for judging feelings as insignificant and unworthy, the self-imposed burden is staggering. Stuffing feelings is a behavior that lacks attention to detail and rapidly develops into a full-blown crusade of taking responsibility for other people.

Everybody has an unforgettable person in life, someone who made a real difference. Rutgar is no different. The first rare individual he experienced was Mr. Phillips. Mr. Phillips not only brought insight and awareness into his life, he helped him think outside the box and look beyond appearances. He's the main reason Rutgar became a detective.

He also had another profound effect, which helped Rutgar work through guilt. Mr. Phillips had a tendency to scold Rocky for everything imaginable, despite the fact he was just being a dog. The first couple of times Rutgar let it slide thinking he'd lighten up, but it never happened. Rutgar felt caught between a rock and a hard place: How could he tell someone he admired that his actions were unacceptable and risk disapproval?

Rutgar felt horrible for not standing up for Rocky. Exhausted from no sleep after a long week of tossing and turning, Rutgar finally risked gently and compassionately expressing his feelings. Paradoxically, Mr. Phillips had no idea he was being critical and appreciated the feedback. He simply wasn't used to the distraction. Dogs were not allowed in the house where he grew up.

The terms "suffering servant" or "martyr" describe the burden of guilt well. Feeling weighted down from heavy doses of self-criticism is an understatement. It's like being personally appointed to carry the weight of the world on your shoulders… and comes down to duty, responsibility and obligation running the show. Trapped in a vicious cycle of self-denial, you're stuck with feeling you owe everybody on the planet.

SELF-JUDGMENT A PROBLEM

Self-judgment is the problem… judgment that a **personal law** has been broken. Throughout life personal laws are established that you come to live by, which turn into a state of conscience or a moral code of conduct. "Break these laws and you'll get caught," guilt condemns. "You cross the line and you're in trouble," it threatens. Feeling guilty is always the penalty. A pulsating heart and thoughts racing at a hundred miles an hour prove the point.

Rutgar helped Matt, now a single Dad, survive his divorce. His case required a few select pictures to be taken of his ex-wife to prove allegations in court. Despite the betrayal, Matt being a nice guy, felt sick inside for his children and himself. He was aware he wasn't perfect and wondered what he could have done differently.

124

Notwithstanding the proof obtained, he questioned if such drastic measures were necessary to gain custody. Even Rutgar's knowledge and mentoring skills couldn't keep Matt from destructive self-talk and harsh internal judgment of this situation.

Face it, deep conditioning convinces you that you are bad and must suffer despite trying every trick in the book to absolve yourself. By making empty promises you'll never keep, you find innovative things to do to fool yourself into believing you can beat taking the rap for your actions.

Some people justify predicaments by what they must do for the sake of others... specifically children or parents. They judge by what they have been taught about God and the Bible; blame their circumstances on money or where they live. No matter what the explanation, it's still an excuse. You are the sole creator of the heaven or hell you experience. Guilt keeps you living in Misery. You've banished yourself to an unholy place by a lack of determination to figure out if past beliefs apply to who you are now.

THE NEGATIVE EGO AT WORK

Suppressing then judging feelings is how the negative ego swindles you into submission. Its primary goal is to make you buy into shame. Trapping you in its clutches by replaying derogatory situations, it reinforces those demeaning times you felt wrong, miserable and inadequate, reminding you you're not worth a plug nickel. As long as the negative ego keeps you judging your behavior you won't move forward. That's its job.

Drinking and partying were not big on Rachel's agenda. One night she went clubbing with a group of friends and in spite of feeling she had had enough alcohol, she overruled her intuition and kept drinking. Her hidden flirtatious and amorous side rose to the occasion and she woke up in bed with her buddy, Jonathan, the next morning. To this day she feels guilty (upset with herself) and when the group gets together neither one of them will make eye contact. (P.S. Her buddy, Jonathan has issues around this too!!)

Think of the times you've been surprised by your own actions. They made no sense. Not having a lick of understanding as to why you did or did not do something... even though stringent training labeled particular actions right or wrong, you did them anyway.

Rather than feel guilty after the fact, be honest about the way you reacted. Watch what you are doing and observe why you are rebelling. A sincere look within gives credence to the fact that you'll try anything to avoid what's actually going on emotionally. You will justify decisions any way you can, finding all kinds of reasons to stay put. More often than not you've been led to take action before but refused to budge.

An outdated hypnotic belief or concept that no longer fits is clamoring for attention. Truthfully, in this instance, the only "sin" (a Greek word for missing the mark, an error made with a bow and arrow in ancient times) you can ever be guilty of is trivializing anger. Not challenging why you suffer is the first mistake. The second is accepting and living with it. Guilt's sole commandment is, "Thou shalt stay in hell." There's a strong message here. **Learn from guilt.** Don't cultivate more of it.

FEAR OF PUNISHMENT

Social order promotes the expected rather than teaching us to be individuals (undivided within ourselves). What actually creates guilt is a fear of being punished for doing what you want, stepping on toes or fear of going against the grain. You've been brainwashed not to question or challenge root beliefs. Question them and you are bad… blight on the landscape of life, making fear of repercussion far outweigh sensibility.

Think of all the people who give up personal wants and desires during the holidays for the sake of family. Are you one of them? Many special occasions are fraught with residual resentment. Too often those gathered are only there because they feel they have to be. During the festivities a whimsical remark is invariably made reminding guests their presence is a mandatory requirement, shedding light on the truth of the situation.

Rutgar howled as he remembered the time his cousin Greg invited his new girlfriend to have Thanksgiving Dinner with the family. His six-year old nephew was supposed to be seated by his grandmother at the of the head table. When the boy's mother tried to put him in the chair beside her, the six-year old adamantly shouted out with complete defiance, "I'm not sitting beside that old lady, she's mean," and confidently stomped into the kitchen. Greg later admitted that what his nephew said was the unvarnished truth... everyone knew it and had to hide their laughter. They all put up with her year after year and the child was the only one who was being honest.

As the six year-old already expressed, you are not here to suffer by putting up or shutting up. Yet that is exactly what happens when deep-seated feelings are set aside. A complete surrender of personal wants, desires and needs is expected. Minor levels of frustration rise to staggering heights. Pressure makes the choice to live in Misery substitute for telling the truth. This leaves you feeling picked on, worn down, used and abused. Guilt rears its head wherever you deny self-worth or refuse to be important. Just "bottle it up and suffer."

Where do you think illness, high blood pressure, depression and anxiety disorders come from? What do you think triggered shootings at schools, the Post Office and McDonalds? Why do you think at least two high-profile ministers slipped over the edge with prostitutes, and what about the recent mess with Catholic priests? Denial doesn't work. Take the time to review why being honest is distasteful. Permanent relief is impossible until you acknowledge what's troubling you.

CYCLE OF GUILT

We've all been taught, and taught well, how we're supposed to behave. We are trained to fit in via custom, religion, parents, teachers, etc. To "get along" we are programmed very early on to do what is right, not to follow how we feel. Seldom is anyone taught to have his own opinion or stand on his own two feet.

Rebecca and Dean are close friends of Rutgar's. Recently they came over to play with Rocky but mostly were seeking reassurance. During the two years they've been married they have spent lots of time shopping for their new home, redecorating and enjoying many weekend getaways with each other. Both Rebecca and Dean believe in a Higher Power, which they feel has guided them to take pleasure in each other's company. This time together has expanded their awareness of the all-encompassing scope of Love "It" includes. They have acted in accordance with their beliefs and are both very much at peace with their mutual decision to miss some services. On the other hand their parents feel participating in every service is an integral part of religious values. They call regularly to chat and without fail check on their attendance. No matter what is said during the conversation, that one question continually leaves a bad taste in their mouths.

Being different is risky. It creates problems. You don't want to go along with the herd but you're drawn into doing what everyone else does. You feel right and wrong at the same time. These feelings are very perplexing and how guilt develops... wanting to fit in and break free at the same time is confusing. A shrewd fellow once commented, "Compromise makes a good umbrella but a poor roof." Staying quiet fortifies the belief that what's being felt is not warranted or valued, making matters worse. Confusion turns into martyrdom, a self-imposed skill that replaces the ability to choose wisely or freely.

People determined to be "good" justify stuffing their feelings with these popular excuses: "What if I hurt his feelings?" "What if she gets mad at me?" "What if he doesn't like it?" "I don't want to upset anyone." "Don't worry. It's okay." "I did that for you." "You owe me because." "I don't want to be a problem." "Oh, don't bother." "It doesn't matter." This is a poor way to escape reality, don't you think?

Guilt is an absolute waste and discounts the vital importance of standing firm; it teaches that what is mandatory (feeling) is dispensable. Guilt keeps your life in a ceaseless holding pattern and guarantees an unsettled stomach, sleepless nights, stress and a dangerous amount of anxiety that medication never cures. Stop the excuses if you want to remove guilt from your life. Quit defending what drives you nuts. The fact that you struggle speaks volumes. Make a sandwich with manure and tell yourself its roast beef. See if it changes the taste.

ESCAPE FROM GUILT

Let's say you're ready to finally end the senseless guilt trips, to stop suffering and be free to do as you please. You are determined to stop living through other people's opinions and enjoy life. How do you go about it?

First: Remove the words "I feel guilty" from your vocabulary and replace them with the words "I feel angry" or "I feel resentful". This allows the **truth** to surface. **Second**: Consider the situation realistically. Where do you feel **forced** to accept what isn't okay, forced to do what you are "supposed" to do rather than doing what **you** want? Be exact and factual about this. Get really, really honest with yourself. **Third**: Do some interior scrubbing. There is an infraction going on... deal with it openly. The sheer relief that comes from acknowledging the truth inwardly is astounding. **Fourth**: Be alert to every ground-in automatic impulse to feel responsible, feel you owe somebody, feel undeserving, feel it's your fault, feel wrong, feel not good enough, ad infinitum. Stop the vicious cycle! Guilt thrives on ingrained behaviors that tell you "no" or that you "owe." It's not true. **Fifth**: Delve into your feelings thoroughly and risk owning them without any cover-ups. "What is **actually** going on here?" is a relevant question to ask. **Sixth**: Follow your intuition. It will NEVER steer you in the wrong direction regardless of appearances to the contrary. This is not to say anxiety won't be present but at least you'll be headed toward freedom. **Seventh**: Risk being IMPORTANT! You **must** learn this one. That's why you are here.

Don't let guilt destroy you. Make better choices. Who do you want to be? The time has come to say goodbye to guilt, which also happens to be the title of a well-written book by Jerry Jampolsky, M.D. Break free and live today as if it's your last.

SUGGESTED STARTING POINTS FOR LEAVING MISERY BEHIND:

1) Stop being responsible for everything and everyone.
2) Watch how frequently you say, "I'm sorry" out of habit.
3) If the mood doesn't strike you, don't do it.
4) Give up believing it's always your fault.
5) Force yourself not to apologize for anything for one day.
6) See what the payoff is for stuffing your feelings and suffering.
7) Allow yourself to matter.
8) Refuse to believe you owe anyone anything for one week.

Chapter 10

Anger, Resentment and Blame

Rutgar had witnessed every conceivable emotion surrounding these topics. They formed the basis for his line of work. "Not to mention receiving a little help from you," he said to Rocky who was snoring quietly by his feet. "You've given me plenty of opportunity to burst at the seams when you act out. The shock I've felt walking in the door after you've ripped things to shreds from lack of attention, quickly puts these three emotions into perspective."

*Rocky perked up, barked in response and playfully grabbed Rutgar's pant leg. "Yah little man, it's like you intuitively know what I'm talking about," he said expressing amusement. He had read between the lines and he came to a startling conclusion, "I'm convinced the reoccurring theme of all three is **control**. People don't ignite unless they feel thrown from a loss of power or a sense of helplessness… of that I'm certain." He looked at the pile of notes he had pulled together. "They're thorough. I can relax and rest assured rewriting Misery's Rule #10 will be relatively simple. Explaining how anger, resentment and blame function is just the ticket to show the people of Misery a way out."*

"Most people walk around like they are sitting on a powder keg and an insane man is holding the match," laughed a policeman who recently befriended Rutgar. Anger, resentment and blame are at a collective all-time high. Road rage is now a common term. Countries large and small have their own nuclear bombs. Who can forget the horrific event of September 11? Murder and abuse are rampant. Divorce rates are soaring. Too many laws strangle our independence. Headlines about the lack of corporate ethics and integrity can't be ignored. Nobody wants to take responsibility.

It is always the other guy's fault. Never yours. As a general rule, somehow someway there's somebody else to blame. It only takes seconds to conjure up rational explanations. Don't step up to the plate and accept the mess you have allowed yourself to get into. This is a solid fact for everyone at some point in life. Say it isn't true... the story below summarizes it well:

WHOSE JOB IS IT?

There were four people named Everybody, Somebody, Anybody and Nobody. There was an important job to be done and Everybody was asked to do it. Everybody was sure Somebody would do it. Anybody could have done it, but Nobody did it. Somebody got angry about that because it was Everybody's job. Everybody thought Anybody could do it but Nobody realized that Everybody wouldn't do it. It ended up that Everybody blamed Somebody when Nobody did what Anybody could have done.

That's the plight of mankind: the refusal to take responsibility. No matter how strongly you disagree, no one can fix your life but you. Blame and resentment won't help. They make matters worse. After all, who is seeing, hearing and feeling there is something wrong? The answer is... nobody but **you!** Since the answer is always "me," guess who gets to do the work? You are the sole one in charge of your life. Let's say you could change everyone in the world, they can revert back in the blink of an eye... the only consistent factor in your life is you.

EMOTION ALARM

No matter what sets it off anger activates a loud internal siren that serves as an early warning system. There's a storm coming and it works like this: A violation occurs triggering emotions. Resentment rushes in appearing as a loss of control, feeling vulnerable, exposed or caught off guard. This escalates what's **already** stewing, what's **already** milling around inside. Then a more forceful feeling takes over and shouts, "danger!" For a split-second you're forewarned, but that's quickly overridden by the urge to strike.

Instead of being alert and catching this right away you hook into feeling powerless and out of control, then react by attacking. The pressure takes its toll whether the attack is silent and held in or spewed out. Those knee-jerk reactions act as loud alarms going off to indicate areas where you feel threatened, where a sense of urgency begs for attention.

Whenever anger, resentment or blame control your life you ultimately admit helplessness, believing you are at the mercy of extenuating circumstances. You admit to being stuck with no way out. It's a declaration of no personal power or ability to solve the predicament, resulting in a conviction to suffer. A little child having a temper tantrum is a perfect example. The child is unreasonable when he doesn't get what he wants. Feeling out of control he kicks and screams, projecting those feelings onto someone else, refusing to listen to reason or take responsibility. The resulting outburst reduces anyone who accepts this kind of behavior as their lot in life to emotional ashes.

Remember, that is reacting, not responding. (As mentioned before, react means to re-in-act, re-create, to do again and its source is the negative ego.) Responding is rooted in choice and self-confidence. Reacting stems from automatic unconscious behaviors that have become ingrained from feeling a lack of self-worth or lack of power. The net result is additional frustration and misery. You either take action to fix problems or problems take charge of you.

Rutgar could not forget Sgt. O'Malley, an intense no-nonsense Anger Management instructor who said it like this: "Don't pay your power bill, then try watching television or turning on the lights. The lack of electricity isn't the power company's fault. You didn't act when it was necessary. Go ahead and blame the system for your oversight or irresponsibility anyway. Tell everyone you know how terrible the electric company is. Have the nerve to shun responsibility and obstinately blame somebody else, but it won't help. It won't change anything. Responding will. It ends conflict. Reacting perpetuates it. The option is yours."

IS ANGER CONTROLLING YOU?
Every time you feel betrayed, belittled, mistreated, over-powered, or tyrannized you reject yourself. Instead of standing firm and self-assured in who you are... you become putty. Look at road rage for example, it's staggering how many people are outraged and blow up when cut off on the freeway. They honestly think it's personal and it makes a lot of them very touchy. Do you really believe the person in the other car knows who you are, specifically picking you out to deliberately ruin your day? It's doubtful, yet by reacting that way you relinquish control.

Instead, try asking yourself why this was drawn to you and then question how a problem can be stuffed so far down that an absolute stranger causes you to blow. It isn't a random occurrence. Maybe you're feeling angry, maybe you're tired of being polite, maybe you're feeling scared, or just maybe you're fed up with all those jerks in the world and want to do them in. Bam! The next thing you know you're facing it... only it's coming **at** you instead of **from** you. This a good time to take the "bull by the horns" and realize that un-dealt with emotions inside, are showing up outside. The exterior is a reflection of the interior. The situation is **simply a trigger**.

Another source is expectation. Expectation is a "subtle" condition that more often than not leads to anger and disappointment. It has to. Be prepared for it to test you frequently. It points out why placing your worth in another's actions leaves you feeling exposed and empty. You hand over control to another and your life isn't yours any more. Expectation puts demands on the future and dictates how things are supposed to be. There's no room for flexibility. After all, things **do** change. Expectation says, " I'll be happy if you just do what I want." Nobody in his right mind wants that job. People aren't meant to be mind readers. The result has to be anger for everyone involved.

Rutgar's undependable cousin Mack quickly came to mind (he has to use him sometimes in emergencies to walk Rocky.) Mack's story ties in with a fascinating book Rutgar read by Harvel Hendrix about couples - explaining how expectation leads to anger in most relationships. Mack made a promise to Hilary and broke it. Hilary felt offended, became withdrawn and was hurt. But, underlying this issue was the fact she had built up an expectation. A typical response regarding the situation is that a promise was made and not kept... justifying her pain. Yes, that is the case but as the author said, "You can only hope other people fulfill their promises. If they don't, you have to deal with the sparked feelings about how this tripped you up and why. In actuality it's revealing an unhealed wound, not something trying to punish you." (Read Chapter #8 again to understand more fully.)

WHO IS IN CHARGE?

We're seldom trained to recognize that each of us has dominion over how we experience the world. That is why there are millions of differing perceptions. You are either in command of emotional reactions (which are tied directly to your mind) or they possess you. Handing the reigns over to another or countering with antagonistic behaviors is guaranteed to keep the chaos rolling and creates a volcanic environment. The stage is set for the day it explodes and reveals itself in a fit of rage.

Rutgar couldn't forget these jarring words from the Anger seminar: "Too few of you question what causes your anger. You just buy into it, go along for the ride and are of the opinion it's not your fault. You're not taught why you're angry or what it can show you. You're merely told it's wrong. As a result this produces a deeply ingrained rule causing you to withhold those emotions. They become repressed and after a while the buried resentment makes you blame others. It's got to go somewhere." As they cheerfully walked out the door Rutgar glanced at Rocky and comically remarked, "At least you're free from the pitfalls of emotional baggage."

When anger threatens, be daring. Don't put up a wall. Seek out what it is that anger, resentment and blame are pointing to. Identify what is hidden beneath the surface. Examine where you feel short-changed. Underneath displeasure lies important evidence. A wise soul once said, "In every adversity lies the seed of equal or greater benefit." Most people are stubborn or too frightened to act. It usually takes life turning upside down, emotional breakdowns or bottoming out before individuals seek answers or insight takes place.

The barrier to achieving this difficult task is that rationally it looks like it's the other person's fault, making the line of reasoning just explained hard to swallow. (See Chapter #7 to understand this concept better.)

A plane flew overheard jogging Rutgar's memory about the time his unassuming Aunt Amanda was standing in line at the airport ticket counter. The fellow ahead of her was being obnoxious, yelling and mistreating the airline employee. He didn't care if he was making a scene. She was upset and embarrassed by his behavior. She would never do that. As she watched she became increasingly uncomfortable, but her discomfort oddly turned to curiosity. Why did this scene make her uneasy, especially since it had nothing to do with her? Using this situation to her advantage she owned her feelings, then examined them in detail. What surfaced was the ability to see into that part of her that was buried away... that part that wanted permission just **once in a while** to act out when she felt irritable or out of control... **AND**, be okay with it.

Amanda had an angry father. Witnessing his behavior made her never want to show her anger. She was afraid of coming across like he did. Consequently, she avoided confrontation and usually kept her mouth shut. After some soul-searching, she also realized that on a few occasions she had acted out in the past, judged herself for it and stuffed it away. She figured out that she needed to promptly forgive herself and let it go.

The same holds true for the guy who flew off the handle. He attracted a soft-spoken, kind, gentle, patient, warm, friendly type. That kind of person pushed his buttons to the max and escalated his anger. He saw that person as wishy-washy and gutless. The key here is that we attract what we need to learn. He's faced with learning to be more sensitive, tolerant and compassionate. "The answer to what bothers you is always inside awaiting recognition," she thought. "Wow, those psycho-babble conversations with Rutgar finally make sense to me."

ANGER AS A TOOL

Learn to take care of yourself. Realize anger is an important feeling. The clincher is to use it strictly as a tool, a technique to catch problems. It's not meant to fortify resentment or blame. See what it is trying to tell you. If you are smart you won't hold onto it. Feel it. Allow it. Make peace with it and release it.

137

Anger is not appreciated for the gift it is... a sore spot needing attention or a reflection of something that is stuck. Nor do you realize that by holding on to it you give it value. It operates as a shield that provides the distance necessary to keep you from facing what's being avoided. According to the standard societal rule "Anger is Wrong," angry feelings you have experienced must be cast off... you were taught they aren't permissible.

The way to handle the road rage scenario is to feel your feelings. Scream, yell, hurt or cry in the car, but realize this person only **triggered** what's already trapped within. Acting crazy by joining the chase at 90 miles an hour won't help. You both may end up dead. Take a glimpse into the feelings it brings up. Do you feel stupid, blind-sided, taken advantage of, or mistreated? This situation only scratches the surface. If you have the stomach to stare it in the face, a gift is hidden in its midst.

Howard, Rutgar's passive client, just lost his job. He complained that he has lots of bills and a great deal of fear right now. He told Rutgar that he feels totally out of control. His throat is tight. He burst into tears the other night and resents his employer. He wanted advice. Rutgar suggested that the first order of business was to feel his feelings in their entirety (in private). Give it all he's got. Go for it full blast emotionally. Allowing whatever he can bear in one sitting, like he did by crying and giving himself permission to feel bitter. Feeling the hatred, anger, pity, need to attack, etc. is a good beginning. This is genuine, lets off steam and encourages acceptance of crucial emotions.

That's the number one rule; feel your feelings regarding any situation totally and completely. Then Rutgar recommended to Howard that he honestly consider how he felt about the job. Howard admitted he hated it and toyed with finding another one constantly. He daydreamed of doing something more fun, something that fit his personality better. Sadly, he never risked doing anything about it. When he got right down to it, the only reason he worked there was to collect a paycheck. He was biding time. Rather than admit this, he flipped the truth around and was irate that his boss did this to him. "I'll bet it would have been okay if the situation were reversed, if Howard suddenly found another job and quit the company with little

138

notice," Rutgar reasoned. (He had learned that this applies to relationships also... "It's okay if I do it, but not you.")

He reluctantly confessed to Rutgar that he wasn't present at work, that his mind was generally occupied with other things. It seemed easier to ignore the truth that nudged him than to risk change. Regardless of what form anger takes, if you dissect it, you'll inevitably find you weren't listening to your instincts. You procrastinated or let feelings of powerlessness override the need to take action, despite the fact that a nagging voice beckoned you to do something. You wouldn't. Eventually you're bound to suffer the consequences of your refusal to listen.

JUSTIFIED ANGER??

There are situations where people feel justified in hanging onto anger... for instance, victims of rape or violent crime. These people did not ask to be raped or victimized. It's logical that they have a right to feel wounded and angry. Yes, victims of crime or rape certainly have the right to feel violated. BUT, staying in that pit of emotional hatred for the rest of their lives is more destructive.

When the time is right, it's necessary to feel all of your feelings surrounding helplessness. Preferably with a therapist or in the privacy of your own home, sit in the anger again and again... in short limited doses. Do this until it's like watching a horror movie enough times that boredom sets in. Feel it down to your toes. Get the poison out. Allow the bitterness to be released. While this is not easy, it lifts feelings of persecution, defuses the emotional hold and frees a person to live a happier life. Please note: **Doing this exercise in no way excuses what happened. It does** permit an individual to attain distance, let go and move forward. Oprah has had several impactful shows based on this idea. (See Chapter #3 for a more detailed explanation of this exercise.)

Each person has the ability to walk away from an emotional violation stronger and more capable of taking care of him/herself. There is always something to be learned from what happens in life if you are willing. No doubt, it takes tremendous courage **and** works if you will allow it.

FINDING THE SOLUTION

Whatever you find infuriating is there precisely to be healed, no matter how distasteful. Stop blaming the world for your misfortune and remember that you are responsible for what you see, hear and feel. That can't be said enough. Embrace emotions openly. There is one answer and one solution. Go look into a mirror, it's right before your eyes.

SUGGESTED STARTING POINTS FOR LEAVING MISERY BEHIND:

1) Remember the phrase: One Finger Out Leaves Three Pointing Back.

2) Be honest and confront areas where you hold onto anger or resentment.

3) Don't justify difficulties.

4) Feel your feelings fully, then release them.

5) Let go of the past by conducting an emotional housecleaning.

6) Take responsibility for your feelings and learn to respond calmly.

7) Work toward expressing what you feel without the bitterness.

Chapter 11

Worry

Rutgar bolted upright, aware that something was wrong. He and Rocky had overslept. Panic rushed through his veins as he glanced at the clock. Not only did he have an important meeting to attend, Rocky was running in circles to go out. He felt unnerved but tried to stay calm by taking deep breaths. His client was extremely meticulous about keeping appointments. "Too much to do, too little time," begrudgingly crossed Rutgar's mind. Suddenly everything came to a grinding halt. "Holy Toledo. I need to take my own advice by keeping my cool and responding instead of reacting. Now is a great time to put my own words into practice," he thought. "To use my rewrite of Rule #11 which unmistakably is about **fear**, to stop these gut wrenching feelings, to refuse to be dragged into worst-case scenarios and stay now! Things are never as bad as they seem. Just like that story I heard about practicing patience:"

A man owned a famous stallion that comprised all his wealth. One day the horse disappeared. Looking dismayed his neighbors rushed over and asked him what he was going to do now that his wealth was gone. The man simply answered, **"I don't know. We'll see."** A few weeks later the stallion returned with four beautiful mares following him. The elated neighbors rushed over again to say, "Isn't this wonderful??!! Not only has your stallion returned, you now own four valuable mares which greatly increases your wealth. What will you do with it?" The man quietly said, **"I don't know. We'll see."**

Within two weeks the man's son went out to train the mares for an upcoming horse show. While working with one of the horses, he fell hard onto the ground breaking his leg in several places. As a result the man was unable to train the horses in time. Once again, the neighbors rushed over and said, "This is a calamity. Without a trainer what are you going to do?" The man calmly replied, **"I don't know. We'll see."**

Sometime later the Calvary came through the valley inducting every able-bodied man. This time the neighbors rushed over eagerly and said, "Aren't you lucky? Your son has a broken leg and doesn't have to go to war." The wise man replied, **"I don't know. We'll see."** . . . And so the story goes.

WE ALL WORRY

Like those uptight neighbors, everyone worries. There doesn't seem to be a way out when you're in the thick of it. Thoughts speed through your head at a sickening pace, multiplying tension and anxiety. Self-imposed mental isolation frazzles your nerves like a form of Chinese water torture and makes you feel frantic. Sanity appears to be an elusive memory, something you just can't quite get a grip on. Oh, if the mind only had an "off" switch!

Worry's magnetic hold doesn't miss a single solitary soul. Even though it has no purpose other than to keep us tormented and miserable, we seem magically hypnotized by the incapacitating spell it casts. Left on its own, it rapidly multiplies like rabbits and is soon out of control. You helplessly drown in mental quicksand as it sucks you in. How does something so utterly useless possess such astonishing power?

For starters there's a lot of disjointed constant mental chatter going on. You know the drill. The negative ego is always blasting some form of "what isn't," viciously taunting you by arguing constantly, determined to keep your emotions in an uproar. Watch it. Your vivid imagination is a crutch to avoid staying **now**, quickly jumping ahead and wondering what's next. Instead of taking a second to calm down and let the dust settle... you seek immediate relief by stressing over every outcome you can dredge up.

Rutgar started to breathe easier. The meeting with his client ended early (wouldn't you know, Mr. Meticulous was late) and he had plenty of time to throw the Frisbee for Rocky.

THE DREADED "WHAT IF'S"

The major difficulty lies in letting the negative ego cart you off to the barren wasteland of "what ifs". Panic combined with a strong urge to figure things out makes you take off like a horse at the starting gate. You are firmly convinced that a limited, irrational squawk box steeped in fear can predict the future! Anxiety-riddled thinking adds to the problem. You take delivery of the goods, buy the farm and then desperately try to dig your way out. And, you do it to yourself. As Mark Twain said, "I have been through some terrible things in my life, some of which actually happened."

Picture a calm lake early in the morning when it's quiet, before any movement. Then visualize a large rock being thrown into the water... watch the circles move out from the initial splash. That's what happens when you worry. Increased anxious thinking throws more rocks into the water and the next thing you know there's a tidal wave. Those ripples distort clarity; distort the way you see things and the potential for clear concrete answers.

Simple common sense tells you what a quiet mind reflects. Silence is the language of that Invisible Intelligence you cannot see, hear, taste, touch or know. Joseph Joubert expressed it like this, "It's easy to understand if you don't try to explain It." Allow your mind to stay blank, if only for a few seconds. Out of that tiny space it's possible to receive unmistakable direction.

THE INCESSANT PEST

The pessimistic mind is not your friend. On average it's good for performing tasks and to keep you from repeating a few mistakes. Other than that it's nothing but a twenty-four hour non-stop irritation composed of intellect, which is not necessarily **intelligence**. It operates as an analytical, emotion-filled storage unit based solely on past/future calculations guaranteed to heat up an already brewing caldron. Composed of ignorance layered upon ignorance, it tricks you into believing that it is knowledgeable, delighting in playing games with your psyche. The pendulum swing of emotions whips you back and forth, keeping the focus far away from **right now**, like a tennis ball in a heated match.

144

Admit that you don't have any idea what the future holds and that truthfully, worry is only a form of guessing. Potential decisions are bound to be based on past experience and must produce similar results. It's a repeat of ancient history coming around for you to look at in another form. Like "re-gifting"... putting a gift you've received into a new box with different wrapping.

There's no doubt problems resemble a huge sinkhole when you're down in there with them. That's why you have to get some distance and refrain from any judgment for a while. Worry feeds on itself and pushes away solutions. You must raise yourself higher than the level of the problem to solve it and that is exactly what staying **now** does. It's the pause that refreshes. While it doesn't make rational sense, when you let go and rest in **now**, alternative plans can surface. The trick is remembering to do it and then making it a new habit.

*Here's an exercise Rutgar uses frequently to calm down and relax his mind. Thinking about Rocky makes this easy: Whenever you feel concerned, scared or panicky, catch yourself. Stop the frenzied thinking dead in its tracks. Act as if a little child or animal just ran in front of your car. It's a fast and simple way to be **now**.*

As a test, write down your thoughts for five minutes and see if they make any sense. You will see that an agitated mind jumps all over the place projecting unlimited pitiful pictures and persuades you to live in mortal fear of your own creations, never questioning their reality. It's scary... yet you listen to it. The mind convincing you to eat that delicious piece of cake is the same mind quickly making a U-turn, bitterly attacking and berating you about the extra pounds you'll have to lose. The mind telling you you're wonderful is the same mind that convinces you you're weak and stupid.

The negative ego keeps you in constant turmoil, thriving on nervous energy... *parallel to watching Rocky madly going after those pesky fleas. "The scratching, biting and licking drives us both crazy until he finally gets dipped at the vet."* It hates a quiet mind. A quiet mind offers no chaos to chew on and no chaos means death to the negative ego. Quietness kills it. Like darkness when light enters a room, it disappears. In order for the negative ego to stay healthy and alive it must make you worry.

LEARN TO <u>NOT</u> KNOW

As an experiment, put two dice in your hand. Despite rolling them for years you're going to have a limited amount of combinations. Something new has to be added, another die, for a different series of numbers to be created. The same is true with life. You must step back from the known for new things to appear. Remember the attitude of the wise man in the stallion story. His willingness to live in the moment and **not know** enabled him to feel safe in the "here and now" without a lot of worry and fear. He went along with whatever was happening doing what he felt led to do... although that is easier said than done when you are in the middle of it.

Rutgar decided to be sneaky. "Those people in Misery can't hear this stuff enough." He couldn't help but reiterate a few themes from Chapter #3 on Fear. Being cagey he expressed them in a slightly different manner, determined to get these points across.

Worry strikes when you stray from the present and the cynical mind goes off on a tangent. If you can, pause long enough to remind yourself that whatever is being thrown at you is **not happening this second**. Refuse to let the despicable mind move you into fast forward or send you on a wild goose chase. Refuse to worry about something that has absolutely no tangible existence... this offers a smidgen of peace. Feeling worried is a clue that you've slipped into never-never land, allowing that inconsistent, chaotic, irrational claptrap to take control.

If you receive shocking news don't be tempted to jump the gun. **Make yourself back off.** Give it a rest... take a deep breath and wait. Begin saying to yourself repeatedly, "I don't know, we'll see." Or, "what has this got to do with me right now?" Or, "am I going to ruin today by thinking about tomorrow?" **Be persistent**. Worry is **always** based on past or future speculation and cannot possibly beat you down unless you leave the immediate moment and cave in to it. It's the only time you are susceptible.

Rutgar got tickled and had to laugh, "I know a few businessmen who would be much better off, if they could just stop thinking things to death. The cartoon strip 'Dilbert' is great at pointing that out."

Worry is always focused on something that doesn't exist, something that might happen or did happen, overlooking the present moment, the **here** and **now**. If you are worrying about past predicaments forget it, they're over and done. You can rehash the situation till doom's day but that won't change what happened. At least learn from it if nothing else.

According to enlightened teachers the definition of a miracle is a change of mind, so let go of your death grip on the known. It's miraculous when you do. Typically the mind ends up leading you instead of you leading it, like a dog walking its master rather than the other way around. You scream bloody murder when all along it's you against you. What other mind does it to you? Driving yourself nuts by needlessly worrying makes you miss the beauty of **now**; miss the very thing that's precious and valuable.

NOW IS PERFECT

When you start with **now** and **stay** there your "little bitty tape-playing mind" won't find an audience. It won't find anywhere to penetrate and infiltrate. Being **now** is the most effective action you can take. It charts a course for a new and exciting life. In his book <u>Awareness & Tranquility</u>, William Samuel wrote, *"Now is perfect. Now is new. Now is clean, fresh and immaculate. Nothing about this very present Now exists because of human history. Now is what it is because Now has nothing but Now to know."* Memorize this and repeat it to yourself often... put it on your mirror or refrigerator.

Truly helpful solutions come out of a **quiet** desire-less mind, out of nowhere. You were led to take action for one reason or another. No matter what the size or significance, **real** answers are spontaneous, often profound and unexpected. Desires, expectations and needs tend to trip you up. They become more important than life itself. Instead of being nice additions these external things become demands for happiness.

LET GO AND LET THE UNIVERSE WORK

The Universe is a wonderfully orchestrated place and works extraordinarily well without any input from you. You don't make yourself breathe, blink your eyes, or digest your food. Something invisible does that, not you. And with the same precision that it operates your body this invisible principal will operate your life... if you let it. Grace is always a surprise. Minus your personal handiwork, glimpses of Life's unlimited potential are yours. Do you honestly believe the Universe doesn't have your best interests in mind? We all trusted as children. What went wrong?

Instead of obsessing about getting the things you want, recognize that ideas drifting into your mind are complete in consciousness already; they could not show up otherwise. It's like a "Coming Attraction" at the movies. You didn't envision it. It came to you on its own. Acknowledge that fact. A dormant tree in winter is barren and looks as if nothing is happening... all the while there is a continual flow of energy, motion and life stirring within. Things aren't always as they appear. The same invisible force that planted the idea in your head will ultimately carry it out. Let it go and leave it alone. Move on to something else. Forget it for a while... stop fretting about how and when.

Rutgar was weeding the yard when he spotted Rocky gleefully rolling on his back in the grass. He paused to snap at a fly and continued lazily taking in the sights. Rutgar leaned against a tree and thought, "Rocky doesn't have anything to worry about. Animals simply live from moment to moment. No wonder they are so content."

*Watching Rocky transported Rutgar's mind back to the people of Misery. He couldn't wait to pose these questions: "When was the last time you actually appreciated the blue sky, the colors of a rainbow or a gentle butterfly? How long has it been since you actually looked at the trees, noticed nature's wondrous array of colorful flowers or smelled freshly cut grass? How often do you actually listen to and hear the sound of birds or crickets?" He was clear it only happens in the **now**; you can't make it happen. You can't save it. You can relish it though. Since what you focus on expands why don't the citizens of Misery use this rock-hard piece of advice to change their viewpoints? This isn't air-fairy patronization, but **solid fact**.*

PRACTICAL STEPS FOR TAKING CONTROL

You are not a hostage of your mind. Use it as a tool to slow down that incessant drivel. Turn it back on itself... take back your power. Whenever that senseless prattle begins, consciously pause to ask it these questions: "How do you know that?" "Is it a fact?" "Is it a reality right here and right now?" "Is this written in stone?" "Does it have to be this way?" When it kicks in again, start asking: "Who told you that?" "How do you know?" Keep at it as long as necessary. This technique defuses the negative ego's intensity because you are willing to defy it, to quit helplessly running from it and confront it. Paradoxically, when you give the mind attention it shuts up!

Risk not reacting for a change, respond instead. Sit back and force yourself to wait patiently for internal answers... this is smarter and a much more efficient way to handle problems. They will appear. That split second pause you took paves the way. Be revolutionary and allow something innovative into your life. You are still teachable; you can still learn.

Another simple exercise that yields quick results is to act as if the obnoxious babble is on a CD, video or audiotape playing in your head. In your minds eye, throw the disk into the woods like a Frisbee or pull the video or audiotape out, destroy it and throw it away. Picture yourself burning a new CD. Insert the CD, a blank video or audiotape and fill it with something that helps build you up and develop your self-esteem... it's your choice. Do this repeatedly... the mind will quiet down in no time.

When the going gets rough Rutgar found simple techniques like these are a tremendous aid to diminish worries or make them disappear. It's important to take whatever small steps you can. Remember, it takes lots and lots of practice. You are irreplaceable and special... the only way that "monkey-mind" beats you up is if you let it.

You aren't the mess you think you are, nor are you helpless. As the song says, "Don't worry, be happy." It may sound like a flippant attitude but in truth it is just that simple. Odette Pollar made this compelling statement, "Embrace change. It's going to happen whether you like it or not."

<u>Suggested Starting Points For Leaving Misery Behind</u>:

1) Experiment... watch your thoughts and how erratic they can be.

2) Doubt and question what the mind tells you.

3) Live in the present moment.

4) Don't project into the future.

5) Ask yourself if what you are thinking is fact or mere speculation.

6) Remember, there are no problems in **Now**.

Chapter 12

Risking

Rutgar was excited. This was going to be a great day! As he and Rocky strolled through the neighborhood soaking up the delicious scents of early morning air he was overwhelmed by feelings of gratitude. Not only had he collected the contents of his trusty notebook, "Simple Practical Ways To Get Out Of A Mess or Another Way To Look At Problems," he had lived what those pages prescribed to the fullest and was sharing it.

"We're really lucky, Rocky. We take risks and reap the rewards. You dig under rocks in the yard. I dig under the rocks in my life. What a team of explorers." Rocky, thrilled to be outdoors with his master, barked in agreement. He felt upbeat too and happily pranced along, tail swinging from side to side, stopping to smell anything that crossed his path.

Rutgar was ready to polish off the final chapter of his replacement kit. "Rule #12 is about Risking, which I've discovered undoubtedly makes people feel **threatened.** *The last important step of this project is to prepare the people of Misery to go out and dive into life."*

He dug furiously through the papers on his desk and discovered a valuable stack he'd saved from a conference on "The Tricky Art of Risk Taking." He felt that they would make a splendid contribution and started to review the informative words while Rocky dozed away on the couch with all four paws in the air.

"The only way out is through," is a significant phrase... something everyone has to accept. Issues don't become etched in unless there's unfinished business.

Predicaments of little concern are handled immediately, and then vanish. Nothing fearful maintains itself unless it's supported. Ironically, that's why it's there.

As Rutgar perused the material he came across these questions and challenged the people in Misery to respond honestly: Do you go to great lengths to avoid someone who upset you? Do you screen calls or not answer the phone? Do you withdraw, fret and worry rather than express yourself? Are you constantly rehearsing what needs to be done, but never doing it? Do you often think, "Oh well, there's always tomorrow?" Are you someone who lives with frequent dread, considers risking to be a chore and the whole idea of taking a chance objectionable?

THE ROAD LESS TRAVELED

It's sad to say but most would answer, "Yes" to the preceding. Even if a situation is uncomfortable it beats trying something new, rocking the boat or possibly failing. Taking care of you ought to be the simplest task in the world. It's not. Wouldn't it be great to be tapped on the head with a magic wand and have all your troubles instantly disappear? **Fortunately** that's not the case. The "road less traveled" is a requirement not an option. It only **looks** like a choice.

Year after year people try initiating change, but the amount of money spent on self-help books, classes and therapy is astonishing compared to the number of people who actually budge out of their comfort zones. Moving forward can't possibly be more frightening than living in silent ignorance. Ignorance in its purity means ignoring the truth.

Each of us is responsible for dispelling our own illusion of fear, like making certain to be de-hypnotized by the magician before leaving the magic show. You have no other choice if you want to be released from the clutches of fear. Seeing into the non-power of imprinted fear-filled beliefs is essential if they are ever to be permanently eradicated. Otherwise they impose arbitrary limits making most people believe change is impossible.

The often-used quote, "Insanity is doing the same thing over and over again expecting different results," accurately describes the residents of Misery. Their lives are dull and routine, empty of adventure. The thrill has gone out of learning and the excitement of risk taking is non-existent. They won't bother with challenging the unknown because a primary requirement for a different life is accepting the cold hard fact that the unexpected is to be expected… they don't like the unexpected.

People fought hard against the idea of planets revolving around the sun, of the electric light and the horseless carriage. If you aren't willing to encounter a few bumps in the road, forget change. It's not going to happen. Change is about taking risks, even if it means the world turns upside down for a while. Galileo, Columbus, Franklin, Ford, Bell, Edison, Einstein and Gates are just a few who questioned the status quo.

Rutgar was aware that taking risks is not only important it's mandatory. "A foreign language isn't mastered without practice," he emphatically declared to Rocky. "Reading or studying a lot of material about change won't cut it. You must practice speaking a new language to prove your proficiency, that you are competent in it. It is also imperative to risk expanding beyond what's comfortable, extending beyond your limits." Rutgar concluded.

THE ULTIMATE WAR

Wars are initiated on the premise of attaining freedom. Freedom is your inalienable right and offers the ability to act in accord with what you believe. With that vision in mind, our forefathers drafted the Constitution. Therefore it would stand to reason if you are following your truth, by definition, you should feel free.

"Rocky, I've listened to enough people to know that most of them don't feel free. They're like a monkey in a rocking chair, constantly moving but never going anywhere."

What happens? The negative ego sets in. Everyone seems to have one, but it's not factored into the equation. It's assumed that people are honest. Over time what begins to surface are greed, need, selfishness and those wanting a free ride. What once exemplified the noblest of intentions falls through the cracks. Take note of all great civilizations. Ideas of freedom were taken for granted and this ultimately led to collapse. So many laws were passed real freedom disappeared… believe it or not it **is** possible to pass too many laws. Freedom is diminished then destroyed. You then have what's called a "nanny state," where the government is the primary care-taker instead of the citizens.

Be alert… the actual warfare begins when you abandon the negative ego's nest. One of the toughest wars you'll ever experience is the war between "you" and "You." The little "s" which represents the negative ego "you," versus the "You" with a capital "S" that eternally **is** freedom. Ingrained beliefs create a rebellion that is supported by the plethora of unwritten laws you operate under. These beliefs fight back. You've been under the negative ego's thumb forever. It's stated well in the Mayor and City Council's motto, "Misery loves company".

The habitual roles you learned to play are just that, "roles" or "scripts." However, you forgot it's only a play. That's why enlightened teachers use the terms hypnotism or nightmare to describe it. No matter how real these patterns or roles seem, the spell must be broken – as mentioned in the beginning they're illusory, something that is blindly accepted and acted out. But, don't kid yourself. It **is** tough and on occasion feels like a horrific battle when serious change is set into motion. This is what starts an inner war. When Misery is left behind there are definitely times when the pain seems unbearable.

The negative ego doesn't want you to leave its clutches, like a dictatorship. It wants to keep you intimidated so you won't venture out. It lets you make progress for a while, allowing some headway, then brings in the heavy artillery. At this stage the question, "Is this all there is?" stands guard like a sentry. (In <u>Illusions</u>, Richard Bach's story about the "Clingons" describes this inner war perfectly.)

GET READY FOR JUDGMENTAL CLATTER
Risking doesn't always go as imagined. Be ready for judgmental clatter to pass through your head like rush hour traffic, convincing you that you can't do anything right and never will. It also resourcefully humiliates you into submission by reminding you of all the mistakes you've made, using specific memories to back up how inept you have been. At this stage the "inner war" is set in full motion and that's where lethargy sets in…*"Cease fire!" Rutgar shouted.*

"This is a good time to reread 'Surrender to Helplessness & Hopelessness' in Misery's Rules & Regulations. It's a definite reminder of what you don't want," Rutgar suggested. Then rigorously rubbing his face with both hands he shot Rocky a mortified look and humbly shared, " You weren't around when I was in high school.

I had a huge crush on Mary Frances and finally got up the nerve to sit by her at lunch. I was cruising up to the table, being very cool, and in a split second slipped on a French fry. The next thing I knew I was flat on the floor and my tray was in Mary Frances' lap. Ugh! It's <u>still</u> hard for me to laugh at that."

You try to thwart the clatter's tiresome ranting but can't, baffled by how this horrible demon of self-doubt ever grew to such gigantic proportions. Rutgar took these quotes directly from his reliable notebook to prove his point... words that were spoken when his clients were fed up:

..."Staying stuck is easier than taking risks. Trying new things is too hard. Change is threatening and I don't want to be on a sinking ship. After all, just because I know what I need to do doesn't mean I'll do it," a frustrated Ron snapped on the phone.

..."But I feel so confused. This stuff is easy to read and makes sense, but has nothing to do with the REAL world. I can understand it on paper, but trying to live it is another story! I feel immobilized by confusion and it seems impossible to make a decision. How do I know what the right thing to do is anyway?" Leslie managed to say through piercing bouts of tears, anger and self-pity.

Be prepared. There are going to be times when the bottom falls out and you end up feeling like you're climbing a greased pole. **But, don't let that get to you!** That's the negative ego's plan and why being willing to risk change is called the "ultimate war." It plays out like this: You're making progress, feeling gutsy enough to take additional risks... shocked to notice things are finally going your way. It feels great! Little by little you're gaining confidence, feeling valuable and worthwhile.

Then... out of nowhere something grabs you unexpectedly and into the pits you go. You're down for the count, which is intensified by waking up feeling overwhelmed with defeat, doom and gloom. All this new stuff you worked so hard to master flies out the window. It's history. The negative ego wants to demolish any signs of progress. "Seek and destroy" is its only mission. ***"Quick, get back in line. Pronto!*** *This is why I referenced those clients," Rutgar thought. "Their words express it perfectly."*

156

SELF-SABOTAGE (THE PROGRESS KILLER)

Rutgar wanted to be as explicit about self-sabotage as he had been about the negative ego tricks. He understood how it completely undermines self-confidence and why it earned the label "The Progress Killer." If you plan on leaving Misery you had better be on your toes. He dove into his dog-eared notebook and jotted down this precautionary information from several cases:

Brittany faced breaking up with an unsavory fellow. He verbally abused her until she finally broke it off. One Saturday night about ten months later she went through his old cards, letters and pictures and became melancholy and depressed. Regrettably, she ended up calling him and when they talked he couldn't wait to brag about his new girlfriend, rubbing it in with delight. She called Rutgar for support, realizing she wasn't as strong as she imagined. Now it was finally clear why she left the relationship, even though she had to begin the healing process all over again.

Bryant was proud of his job, worked hard to achieve success and was on top of the world. One night he worked late and noticed the boss left his office door unlocked. Bryant was curious about his co-worker's salaries. Earlier he'd noticed the computer printout lying on his boss's desk. After everyone left, Bryant snuck into the office, looked at the confidential information and came out fuming. The other salaries were higher than his. He called Rutgar madder than a hornet. Rutgar suggested he sit in his feelings for a while then respectfully ask his boss pertinent questions about his value to the company. He also reminded Bryant that he had been contented with his job before he saw the other employee's salaries.

Jenny was always trying to lose weight. When she was alone and it seemed like she was making progress the negative ego inevitably chimed in. It whispered suggestions to call one of her parents or a particular friend, neither of which emotionally built her up. Each time she insisted she could handle it. She ended up being upset and down in the dumps. As recourse, she generally spent too much money shopping then ended up at the refrigerator to boot. She knew better but invariably did this anyway. Rutgar assured her at some point she would get fed up with the pain and quit. Until then, he could only listen and encourage her to find strength in herself and practice the various techniques he had taught her.

KEEP TRYING

Be Persistent. When the going gets tough, the tough get going. It feels like you are losing the battle at times, **BUT DO NOT JUDGE THAT!** That's how the war continues. Judgment or reaction gives the negative ego power. Actually, you can use the negative ego's attack as a sign of accomplishment and a way to pat yourself on the back. It never pulls out the heavy artillery unless it's really threatened, which means you must be making progress or it wouldn't attack so viciously.

When this new "You" is deeply seated and fully etched in, when you are brimming with self-confidence and really know who you are, you won't take the bait. It takes two to have a war, the old "you" versus the new "You." "Remember that!" Rutgar reminded Rocky, feeling invigorated as he wrote this section. "It's like watching an action packed movie where everybody cheers for the good guys. In order to win the war you must stand firm!" Rutgar bellowed, startling Rocky. "Sorry little guy. I was so inspired by what I wrote I was thinking out loud."

Rome wasn't built in a day, nor does life change over night. You aren't familiar with freedom... what it's like to be out of Misery. If you aren't hooked by the negative ego you won't get caught... that's freedom. Before long what resembled an abyss turns into paradise. *"Just hang in there and don't give up,"* Sgt. O'Malley often said.

ACTION SPEAKS - READY, SET, RISK!

As author Arnold Patent said, "Look at your life and see what you've got and know that's what you want, because if you wanted it any differently you'd change it." Those who read books, listen to tapes, seek support and attend classes are certainly on the initial path. The next question then is, "What are you doing to put the techniques into action, to utilize what you've learned?" Spouting off good intentions accomplishes nothing.

The old adage "Actions speak louder than words," is true. Words without action are meaningless and ineffective... after a while nobody listens. If you're not going to follow through, don't bother speaking. You're just fooling yourself. Several well-known therapists suggest making a list of everything you want. Then make a second list of what's blocking you. The resulting outcome shows how preconditioned beliefs take priority over possibility. It can be that simple.

JUST DO IT!

Nike developed an advertising campaign enticing individuals to chance participating rather than procrastinating. Their powerful words rallied people to take action, not sit on the sidelines. "Why wait?" they asked. "Put yourself to the test." "Go for what you want." "Don't give up." Worldwide, other companies followed suit and motivational marketing spiked the charts!

Rutgar defined "risking" as surging ahead and overcoming false beliefs by doing things you're afraid to do, were not allowed to do or do not know how to do. This begins by unlearning what's been programmed into you, similar to cult members who must be debugged or deprogrammed. "My rewritten version of Misery's Welcome Kit attests to that. History too. Freedom and risking go hand in hand," he cheered passionately. "To quote Nike, 'Just do it!'"

Need encouragement? Watch television specials, movies or study people who beat the odds. Their determination, perseverance and commitment never allowed them to quit. It's inspiring and uplifting. Like riding a monster roller coaster, the excitement and exhilaration is infectious. Watch "It's A Miracle," on the PAX television network or focus on the dauntless willpower of Christopher Reeve, Lance Armstrong or the countless other individuals whose courage refused to let them give up.

Life is like a faucet. Risk facing fear and life pours out. Shut down and the flow stops. In the movie "What About Bob?" his brave baby steps, baby steps, baby steps started the ball rolling. Risk at least once a day, even if it's small. Feel the satisfaction it brings, the satisfaction of knowing anything is possible.

*"Rocky, I compiled an Appendix for people in Misery who are serious about change. It's made up of a few helpful guidelines to bolster shaky psyches as the journey begins. It contains specific information to spark the imagination and make sure no one is left directionless. I've included a list of "**Suggested Simple Ways To Get Started**" which helped me begin the process of risk-taking; some pertinent material I gathered on "**Areas Most Likely for Self-Sabotage**" to keep people alert to the negative ego tricks that grab everyone; as well as my personal cheat sheet*

called *"Practical Principles"* as a summary of the rewritten Rules & Regulations for an easy reference. This way those courageous people ready to leave Misery behind will be prepared for the challenge taking risks creates. When it's all said and done Rocky, I've worked hard to be thorough. Not only do I want everybody to succeed, I want everyone to realize no matter how bad things seem there is **always** a solution. Life is what you make it! As Benjamin Franklin said, "I never met a problem that couldn't be solved."

Rocky, sensing his master's delight immediately raced over to Rutgar for a tickle on his tummy and a zesty head rub. He gazed lovingly at Rutgar and hopped into his lap. He loved his master and his master loved him. Neither one could be any more content.

With a deep sigh Rutgar relaxed, closed his incredible notebook and tucked it away. He felt pleased and proud of his accomplishment. Rewriting Misery's Rules & Regulations was an eventful undertaking that was well worth his time and effort.

Rutgar stood up from his desk, stretched a bit and signaled for Rocky to follow. "Come on boy, it's bedtime. After a good night's rest we're sneaking back into Misery and completing the final leg of our clandestine scheme." Rocky jumped enthusiastically and barked loudly as they ventured down the hall. "Seize the day!" Rutgar defiantly shouted out.

CONCLUSION
(RUTGAR'S REVENGE)

PART III

It was early morning when Rutgar and Rocky reached Misery. The sun wasn't up yet. Today was the day! The two masked marauders all dressed in black were heading back to Misery to replace their old Welcome Kits with Rutgar's new and improved version.

As they approached the Welcome Center, there wasn't a soul in sight. The Mayor and City Council were too cheap to pay for streetlights, so the duo weren't concerned about being seen. Rutgar wasn't comfortable with breaking into the building, but knew he didn't have a choice. It was imperative! As he reached the door, he jiggled the knob. Amazingly, it wasn't locked! He'd had enough experience to know that when change is on the horizon, nothing gets in Its way. With Rocky in tow, he rushed over to the desk where the Kits were stacked, exchanged Misery's Welcome Kits for his updated version and hurried outside. Rocky stuck close to his side. The dismay on his face showed he didn't like this idea one bit.

It only took seconds for both of them to leap into the car and escape. They couldn't get out of there fast enough! "Whew, Rocky, that really made my heart race. I haven't done anything that exhilarating for years," exclaimed Rutgar. Rocky put his paws on Rutgar's shoulders and excitedly licked his face. They felt relieved. "What a great pal you are little buddy. Who else would have seen me through this arduous task? Let's go home and celebrate!"

As they started the drive home they were greeted with the first light of day. The vast array of brilliant colors emanating from the rising sun touched him deeply. Nothing could have been more beautiful. It was an affirmation of the task he just completed. Rutgar grinned and peacefully thought, "There is boundless beauty in each new day once Misery is left behind!"

Appendix

You have been prepared. Now it's time to try out what you've learned. Practice makes perfect. If you are truly sick and tired of being sick and tired don't wait. Expand your life. It's the only way that what's been taught becomes useful and permanent. Doing things differently is necessary for a life full of new experiences and a variety of new outcomes. Don't be afraid to leave Misery behind!

Rutgar and Rocky

Suggested Simple Ways to Get Started

(Can be used as a check list)

1. Do the opposite of what you are used to doing.
2. Say "yes" when you mean "yes," "no" when you mean "no".
3. Try new foods.
4. Risk smiling at people or saying hello to strangers.
5. Risk giving compliments (that are real to you).
6. Share things with people, let them get to know you better.
7. Allow yourself to be approachable.
8. Risk being more vulnerable and open.
9. Trust your gut on little things then move on to bigger ones.
10. Stop and listen inside for a second at least 20 times a day.
11. Risk telling the truth when you're afraid to.
12. Tell the truth about being afraid to tell the truth.
13. Risk intimacy in small bites, let someone into your life gently.
14. Eat alone in a restaurant.
15. Go on a day trip or vacation alone.
16. Go to see a movie alone.
17. Send restaurant food back if it's not right.
18. Talk to friends and relatives when you feel upset.
19. Ask to speak to a store supervisor or restaurant manager if you're not happy with the service.
20. Send a card or letter as a kind gesture or just for the heck of it to be silly.
21. Let people you care about know that you care.
22. Risk giving hugs to people.
23. Ask for support if you feel down.
24. Call someone you feel concerned about or think could use support.
25. Spontaneously send flowers or balloons.

26. Start a conversation with someone you typicaly avoid.
27. Risk taking a mental health day from work.
28. Leave things undone at your desk or at home in small doses.
29. If you are controlled by neatness leave dishes in the sink.
30. Clean up more often if you are used to being messy.
31. Allow yourself to experience feeling equal with everyone else.
32. When you feel strongly about something, risk speaking out.
33. Go somewhere you've always dreamed of going, even day trips.
34. Call someone that you consider out of your comfort zone.
35. Pay attention when spoken to, really work at being present.
36. Buy yourself something special.
37. Don't buy anything if that's an escape for you.
38. Respond to situations instead of blindly reacting to them.
39. Relax rather than panic.
40. Hang out in an upscale store if inadequacy or money is an issue.
41. Let it out: yell, scream, cuss – alone.
42. Allow yourself to cry when you feel like it.
43. Say "thank you" to anyone who gives you a compliment – accept it graciously without saying another word.
44. Spend quality time with you – plan dates with yourSelf.
45. If you MUST take action (especially drastic action), make certain you are composed inside BEFORE you act.
46. Make new friends, ask someone to have lunch or go to a movie.
47. Don't make lists (if that's a habit).
48. Be late if you are timely (even by only a couple of minutes).
49. Be on time if you are usually late.
50. Get out of habitual ruts - take a different route to work, the grocery store or while running errands.
51. Do something out of the ordinary for yourself each week.
52. Express something that needs to be said (risk first with people who are safest).
53. Compassionately let people know when you are upset.
54. Talk to people who make you feel intimidated.
55. Travel somewhere you don't speak the language.

56. Start a conversation with an authority figure.

57. Tell someone of importance you love or care for them.

58. Let yourself be angry when you feel that way.

59. Don't put up with something that bothers you.

60. Never stop the effort to stretch your boundaries.

61. Go to a large event alone if crowds bother you.

62. Go to a small event if you don't like to stand out.

63. Wear colors that aren't the norm for you.

64. Turn off the TV; turn on music or read.

65. Be alone in silence without any TV, radio or stereo.

66. Tell someone a joke, even if you're not good at it.

67. Reach out to loved ones with smiles and compliments.

68. Let people give to you if you are not used to receiving.

69. Give to others if you are not used to giving.

70. Keep a list of your accomplishments and read it often.

71. Be prepared for the down times, have a support system.

72. Try a new sport or form of exercise.

73. Plant some flowers or grow vegetables.

74. Cook if it's unusual.

75. Entertain socially - plan a dinner party or have people over.

76. Go to a museum, comedy club or community playhouse.

77. Go to a coffee shop then relax, read and people watch.

78. Go to a neighborhood park and observe everything going on.

79. Bake cookies for the mailman, bank teller, dry cleaner or store clerk.

80. Action is essential – keep inventing ways to take risks.

FIND EVERY POSSIBLE WAY YOU CAN IMAGINE TO TAKE RISKS AS **SAFELY** AND AS **SENSIBLY** AS POSSIBLE. IT'S WHAT MAKES LIFE INTERESTING AND EXCITING!

Most Likely Areas For
Self-Sabotage

Rutgar couldn't think of a better story than this one from Aesop's Fables to illustrate the make up of the negative ego: Once upon a time there was a scorpion sitting on the bank of a river. He wanted to cross the water so he asked a frog close by if he would take him across on his back since he couldn't swim. The frog said, "We are natural enemies. If I agree you will sting me and I'll drown." The scorpion quickly replied, "Why would I do that? We'd both end up drowning." The frog thought about it for a minute, then going against his better judgment agreed. When they were halfway across the river the frog felt a horrible pain and knew he had been stung by the scorpion. Before they went under the frog said to the scorpion, "Why did you do that? Now we're both going to die." The scorpion immediately replied, "I just couldn't help myself!"

This tale sums up what we continually do to ourselves by going against our intuition. Stay alert for possible pitfalls of self-sabotage so you won't continue repeating old patterns. Leaving Misery behind is a rough and sometimes terrifying journey, but definitely worth the adventure!

1. Be careful of becoming melancholy when going through old pictures, letters, cards and special songs.
2. Don't over eat, then allow yourself to feel depressed and judgmental.
3. Watch out for partying too hard and feeling ashamed.
4. Don't use the "truth" as a club, i.e. "Let me be honest and tell you…"
5. Don't talk about past relationships with a new significant other.
6. Don't show up unexpectedly at someone's home.
7. Don't embellish or make a situation out to be more than it is.
8. Don't be demanding, pushy or have expectations of others.
9. Make certain old relationships are finished before becoming involved.
10. Don't participate in gossip or listen to it.
11. Avoid third party conversations.
12. Don't call someone who will bring you down or make you feel small.

13. Avoid settling for less than what works for you.
14. If you are tired, in a bad mood or feeling grouchy, don't become involved in deep conversations.
15. Be careful when it comes to isolating or withdrawing too often.
16. If you "just have to" talk to someone, it's usually not a good time for talking.
17. Be leery of giving in or giving up your needs.
18. Before trying to go back to a relationship, thoroughly examine why you left.
19. Don't say "yes" when you mean "no," and "no" when you mean "yes."
20. If getting on the scale is a way you judge yourself, don't do it.
21. Avoid shopping or spending too much money to fill a void.
22. Be wary of bad timing and not following your intuition.
23. Don't lash out and say things you'll regret… count to ten.
24. Don't swim in guilt or carry the burdens of the world.
25. You ultimately pay somehow so don't cheat or have affairs.
26. Don't take on more responsibility than you can handle.
27. Be honest about how emotionally strong you are.
28. Don't try to be "friends" after a break up.
29. Stop inquiring about someone you are no longer with.
30. Don't go through other people's drawers, desks, wallets, personal papers or bills.

Always Check Out Motivation BEFORE You Act: *Rutgar didn't want to go into too much detail, yet he could reminisce for hours about the massive number of clients who got caught up in self-destructive behavior.* Irrespective of the reason behind their actions, that little talking snake (the negative ego) argued them into submission every time, pulling out all the emotional props to keep the nightmare going. Most of us have experienced this phenomenon. It superimposes itself quietly and quickly "in the blink of an eye," determined to have its way. A simple rule to follow is: "If it's underhanded or circumspect don't do it!"

*Rutgar wanted to make it clear that this list is very generalized and to be used **only as a guide**.* It is strictly based on suggestions, and he realized that each individual situation comes with its own unique set of circumstances. The bottom line is to follow intuitive promptings and always be willing to take responsibility for your actions.

Rutgar's Practical Principles

(A Handy Cheat Sheet)

It is NEVER the other guy!

Pointing one finger out leaves three pointing back.

Say "yes" when you <u>mean</u> "yes" and "no" when you <u>mean</u> "no".

Express yourself. Own your truth. **You** are important.

Feel your feelings when they arise. Emotions are signals.

Change will only occur if you risk doing things differently.

Pain is in proportion to the love you withhold from yourSelf.

Don't stuff, analyze or rationalize feelings.

Remember to be Selfish with a capital "S."

What you **resist** persists.

What you focus on expands.

Stay Now!

You are working through <u>deeply</u> imprinted patterns, don't give up!

References and Resources

Books

Scott Adams, *When Body Language Goes Bad*, McMeel Publishing, New York, New York, 2003

Richard Bach, *Illusions*, Dell Publishing, New York, New York, 1979

John Bradshaw, *Healing The Shame That Binds You*, Health Communications, New York, New York, 1988

Susan Jeffers, Ph.D., *Feel The Fear And Do It Anyway*, Ballentine Books, New York, New York, 1988

Joel S. Goldsmith, *Consciousness Transformed*, Acropolis Books Publishing, Lakewood, Colorado, 1998

Harvel Hendrix, Ph.D., *Getting the Love You Want*, Holt-Henry Company, Gordonsville, Virginia, 2002

Gerald Jampolsky, M.D., *Say Goodbye To Guilt*, Love is Letting Go of Fear, Center for Attitudinal Healing, Tiburon, California, 1985

Arnold M. Patent, *You Can Have It All*, Simon and Schuster, New York, New York, 1996

Watty Piper, *The Little Engine That Could*, Penguin-Putnam, New York, New York, 2002

William Samuel, *A Guide To Awareness and Tranquility*, William Samuel Foundation, Mountain Brook, Alabama, 1989

Eckhart Tolle, *The Power Of Now*, Namaste Publishing, Vancouver, B.C., Canada, 2004

Dr. Lawrence J. Peters, *Peter's Quotations*, Quill-Williams-Morrow, New York, New York, 1992

Movies

"Phenomena," Touchstone Studios, L.A., California, 1998

"The Matrix," Warner Brothers Studios, L.A., California, 1999

"What About Bob?" Touchstone Studios, L.A., California, 1991

Classes

Susan Trout, PH.D., Institute for Attitudinal Studies, Alexandria, Virginia

Kay Causey, *The Rest of Myself*, White, Georgia

About the Author

Armed with only her heart and an idea Pat Zerman founded the Atlanta Center for Attitudinal Awareness. The Center has been providing dynamic personal and spiritual opportunities for the past 15 years. As director, Pat counsels, conducts classes and publishes a monthly newsletter. She has produced audio and videotapes and made guest appearances on TV and radio shows. Her dedication, caring and years of experience at the Center continue to positively change lives for those who participate in her classes.

She received her Masters Degree in Counseling Psychology as well as availing herself of countless books written in the self-help field and a broad spectrum of spirituality-based books. Her own difficult life experiences of having an alcoholic mother, the murder of her sister and her stepbrother's death from AIDS pushed her to delve deeply into these writings.

After continual digging, soul searching and lots of trial and error, she found answers to her questions. Through intense pain Pat became willing to apply various tools and techniques to get to the bottom of her issues. The relief this brought guided her to share this opportunity with others. The Center utilizes a specialized form of teaching that quickly gets to the root of problems, which eliminates the need for years of therapy.

Clients learn to risk loving and respecting themselves by taking action. Most individuals don't know how or are too afraid to risk taking this kind of action on their own. People **get honest** about the feelings that run them and are able to work through and dump emotional baggage from the past. She demonstrates the importance of learning to live only **now** and **stop projecting into the future.** Using techniques from Pat's classes individuals begin taking responsibility for their lives, stop blaming, experience their emotions fully and learn to forgive themselves and others.

By showing clients they must come first she boldly goes against the norm. Her approach stresses what she terms Selfishness with a Capital "S," which means that you are all that you've got... never **sell** yourself short. Why? Whenever you sell yourSelf short, life will reflect this right back to you. You end up creating a life filled with considerable discomfort, and you don't realize you're the one responsible.

From the inception of the Center, Pat has witnessed the enormous success of her techniques in changing people's lives. Affectionately referred to as the "Laser Lady," Pat mixes exceptionally accurate discernment with piercing forthright **honesty**. But, as her clients attest, behind her resolute exterior lies a loving, caring and compassionate person who **knows** this works. The results speak for themselves!